Social Dimensions of Canadian Youth Justice

Bernard Schissel

Toronto Oxford New York
OXFORD UNIVERSITY PRESS
1993

Oxford University Press
70 Wynford Drive, Don Mills, Ontario M3C 1J9

Toronto Oxford New York
Delhi Bombay Calcutta Madras Karachi
Kuala Lumpur Singapore Hong Kong Tokyo
Nairobi Dar es Salaam Cape Town
Melbourne Auckland Madrid

and associated companies in
Berlin Ibadan

Oxford is a trademark of Oxford University Press

Canadian Cataloguing in Publication Data

Schissel, Bernard, 1950–
  Social dimensions of Canadian youth justice

Includes bibliographical references.
ISBN 0–19–540837–3

1. Juvenile justice, Administration of – Social aspects –
Canada.   2. Juvenile delinquents – Canada – Social
conditions.   I. Title.

HV9108.S34 1993   364.3'6'0971   C93–094578–6

Excerpts from D. Owen Carrigan, *Crime and Punishment in
Canada* by D. Owen Carrington. Used by permission of the
Canadian Publishers, McClelland & Stewart, Toronto.

Excerpts from Rupert Ross, *Dancing with a Ghost* by
permission of Butterworths Canada Ltd.

Table of Contents

Acknowledgements

Many people have contributed to this book in one way or another. In not burdening the reader with an exhaustive list of these kind people, I have chosen to acknowledge only those individuals and organizations that have directly contributed time, energy, and resources to this manuscript.

To my colleagues/friends in the Department of Sociology and in the College of Arts and Science, University of Saskatchewan for institutional and intellectual support and to the President's SSHRC Research Fund and the University Publications Fund, University of Saskatchewan, for financial support, many thanks. Gratitude goes to Jim Frideres of the University of Calgary for guidance and critical commentary. I would also like to express my gratitude to Nancy Poon, Linda Maj, and Kristina Shimmons for their considerable effort and technical expertise.

I wish to acknowledge my debt to the John Howard Society, Edmonton, Alberta for making their data available to me and for pursuing justice with compassion and insight. Thanks to the Canadian Centre for Justice Statistics for the use of their Relative Trends Data set. Thanks, also, to Oxford University Press and its editorial staff for helping to make this manuscript a reality.

It is traditional to thank families for not making demands while the writing process is taking place. I, however, need make no such acknowledgement. My two sons enrich my life when they do stop me from working and it is to them that I owe my sense of purpose and my awareness that, as I ask that they be treated justly by society, I also must ask that all children be treated justly. Finally, and most importantly, to Wendy for making the writing process something to share. It is to her that I owe gratitude not only for proofreading and critical commentary, but also for support, encouragement, and understanding.

Preface

The Young Offenders Act, implemented in Canada in 1984, was intended to make the youth justice system more like the adult system in which justice was administered on the basis of individual accountability. The primary function of the act was to maintain, for accused young offenders, the right to due process in the courts; theoretically and ideally, the act enabled youth in trouble with the law to confront their accusers. In contrast, the Juvenile Delinquency Act of 1908 generally ignored the legal rights of the accused to follow instead the principle of *parens patriae*. *Parens patriae* was a general philosophical principle emphasizing the special needs of youth because of their state of dependency and development. It underscored the child welfare position, that the state must act as the parent of the child, securing the needs rather than the rights of the young offender. Such a paternalistic social welfare posture stressed control and reha- bilitation, but it de-emphasized the legalistic components of youth misconduct. With the declaration of the Young Offenders Act, the courts were required to pursue due process for young offenders while maintaining the principle of *parens patriae*. These seemingly contradictory demands were accompanied by several other changes which provided for diversion, alternative measures, and rigid guidelines directed at age, access to legal counsel, sentencing, and confid- entiality.

This book is not a comparison of the working of the Young Offenders Act relative to its predecessor. Nor is it a study of the functioning and effectiveness of the youth court system in its complicated mandate. No attempt is made to assess diversion and alternative measures relative to legal processing and sen- tencing. This book, a study of the social nature of youth crime and justice, is based on the following analytical approaches. Firstly, I place the history of youth crime and justice in a socio-economic context and supplement an historical discussion with an empirical analysis of national youth court data. Secondly, I use an empirical, analytical study of one youth court's jurisdictions over a six-month period. The young offenders in this specific analysis are those who are handled by the system in a formal manner. Obviously, the many youth who are processed informally under the social welfare provisions of the Young Offenders Act are excluded. The research upon which this second analysis in the book is based assesses the *quality* of justice experienced by youth who are confronted by the courts; it investigates the legal, court specific, and extra-legal (primary socio-economic) influences that help determine judicial outcomes. In short, the book is a socio-legal study of both the history of justice in Canada and the dispensing of justice in one youth court system with the presumption that, although youth court administration is peculiar to provincial and local jurisdictions, the results have general applicability—given the universal nature of the Young Offenders Act and Canadian jurisprudence. Thirdly, I present a cultural critique of conventional legal systems especially for Native young offenders in Canada.

I have formulated the theoretical arguments in this work on a critical sociology of law paradigm. My basic premise is that the structural position of individuals in society determines privilege, and that those who are placed in a disadvantaged social and economic position receive the least of what society has to offer. In the context of the legal system, certain categories of youth, namely minority and lower-class youth, receive the harshest justice.

The data collected from the youth court jurisdiction in this study have been analysed to determine the relative impact of legal and extra-legal characteristics on outcomes at different levels of justice. The extra-legal variables include race, class, legal experience, and family influence. In general, the critical, sociological analysis attempts to determine whether certain social categories of individuals are treated differentially. This study argues that unequal treatment may be partly responsible for the class- and race-based nature of criminality, and that institutions, such as the law, are as responsible for the production of criminal behaviour as are the influences of individual background or circumstance. Simply put, if youth are treated harshly and unfairly by the system, it is possible that such treatment contributes to a negative and potentially criminal self-image. Although I am not testing a Labelling Theory of youth crime (Lemert 1967), I suggest that by recognizing social and economic bias in the law as it is created and applied, and by discussing bias in the context of the interactionist model of institutional labelling and criminal careers, we might come to a greater understanding of the relationship between individual experience in institutions and subsequent criminal behaviour. Although labelling theory has generally fallen into disfavour for lack of empirical support and for its tendency to downplay individual volition, its basic principles are important and should not be abandoned categorically (Jackson and Griffiths 1991; Gibbons 1987). While this analysis is unable to test the impact of discriminatory treatment on future criminal behaviour, I argue that any study that chronicles bias in the justice system must be cognizant of the implications of harsh treatment on individual character and emotional welfare.

Chapter One presents an historical overview of the theories of youth crime and justice and establishes the theoretical and historical relevance of research on youth justice. Chapter Two discusses the history of youth crime in Canada, and illustrates the social and economic basis of juvenile crime and the administration of juvenile justice. Using official statistics, Chapter Three explores the historical and contemporary trends in youth crime in Canada, and discusses the possible explanations for dramatic historical fluctuations in arrests and convictions. Chapter Four introduces the conflict perspective of youth crime and reviews the literature addressing explanation for discriminatory justice experienced by young offenders. The last section in this chapter addresses the universality and importance of youth misconduct, in light of the critical position that the judicial selection of young criminals is highly discretionary. Explanations of the models used to test a Conflict Theory of youth crime are presented in Chapter Five. Chapter Six provides the results, summary, and conclusions of the youth court analysis. The descriptions of the models are presented verbally and in tabular form, and are based on high-order cross-tabulations presented in the causal format of log-linear techniques, logit analysis. This technique is explained in the methodology chapter, Chapter Five. Chapter Seven is a discussion of how Native culture stands at variance with legal culture, and it offers a plausible explanation as to why certain categories of youth are at a disadvantage in the court system. The concluding chapter, Chapter 8, offers some insights into the present situation of youth crime and punishment, and offers some alternatives to the present court system.

It is important to note that this book investigates both serious and non-serious types of youth crime. Most explanations of crime and delinquency are based on a commission or non-commission dichotomy. It is my concern that such a working definition precludes a clear understanding of the pervasiveness of youth misconduct and the discretionary nature of the scrutiny of such misconduct.

chapter one

Criminological Theory and

Youth Crime

This chapter briefly describes the history of criminological theory with respect to youth crime and justice. Here, I illustrate how the development of the juvenile legal system has been closely associated with the functionalist/consensus criminological theory. Beginning with the conservative origins of consensus theories, the chapter develops a critical perspective on youth crime based on the philosophical legacy of Marxism. It argues, from a critical perspective, that the youth justice system in Canada has responded in a piecemeal fashion to the short-term interests of social policy-makers. The best illustration of the *ad hoc* nature of juvenile justice is offered in the final section, which discusses the Young Offenders Act with respect to social reform.

Consensus Theory and the Functionalist Paradigm

Given the long-standing functionalist tradition in social thought, it is understandable that many of the original sociological theories of crime and delinquency took an order-oriented approach to crime and abnormal behaviour. From the Durkheimian perspective, criminal behaviour was viewed as the result of society's inability to subdue or control man's inherently avaricious nature. The utilitarian stance of classical criminology suggested that these uncontrolled tendencies were antagonistic to rational, normative conduct. From a Structural-Functionalist perspective, unbridled self-interest was viewed as incompatible with societal stability and harmony.

Social Darwinist theories of crime causation preceded structural-functional theories and provided the analogy underpinning structural-functionalism. Social Darwinist theories attempted to reduce the causes of non-conventional behaviour to the biological level, resulting in later theories of crime that viewed lawbreakers as inherently flawed (Sheldon 1949; Glueck and Glueck 1950; Conrad 1963; Eysenck 1977). The interest accorded to Klinefelter's XXY Chromosome Syndrome (Casey *et al.* 1966; Price *et al.* 1967) and the preoccupation with sex chromosome abnormality bore testimony to the desire amongst academics and lawmakers to link crime and biological inheritance. General acceptance of a biological causation model of crime permitted lawmakers to initiate state intervention on the basis of perceived dangerousness of individuals, and of the potential danger involved when certain families created new generations of genetically defective offspring. Specifically, ostensibly bad individuals were scrutinized and punished, not necessarily on the basis of illegal behaviour, but rather on the basis of presuppositions regarding their physical and psychological predispositions. Most of the premises of this deterministic approach fell into disfavour because they lacked empirical validation and were ideologically unsound (Sarbin and Miller 1970; Taylor *et al.* 1973; Shah and Roth 1974).

Inevitably, bio-social and bio-psychological constructions of criminal behaviour were responsible for validating and advocating social inequality. Nevertheless, biological explanations of deviant behaviour have recently resurfaced. Current sociobiological research in alcoholism, for example, concentrates on identifying individuals with high-risk propensities to alcoholism (Pollock *et al.* 1983, Pollock *et al.* 1986; Goodwin 1986). As well, recent work on male predispositions to violence attempts to link evolutionary concepts, such as reproductive competition and status competition, with homicidal behaviour in male gangs (Wilson and Daly 1985). Lastly, recent interest in the taxonomy of sexual offenders (Knight 1988; Knight and Prentky 1987) and the ensuing medical treatment of such offenders (Bradford 1988) is further evidence that the search for the biological basis of bad behaviour continues unabated. With respect to youth delinquency, an interest in biological phenomena is apparent in recent work on the etiology of delinquency (Denno and Schwartz 1985) and in research on the links between hormones levels and adolescent male aggression (Magnussen, Statten, and Duner 1983; Olweus 1983).

The Psychogenic School of criminological explanation, which evolved from sociobiology, maintained many of the deterministic aspects of sociobiology by concentrating on inborn psychological defects for the explanation of non-conventional behaviour. However, the psychogenic perspective also introduced the notion of early childhood socialization as a moulder of personality and behaviour, and consequently endorsed concepts of 'normal family life' and 'domesticity'. Eysenck, for example, argues that the connections of

> absence of father, absence of mother, poor conditions of upbringing, lack of home life, and so forth, with criminality, while interesting, lack any great causal importance because it is difficult to see just precisely how these various factors exert their influence. It is hoped that, by relating these factors to a general theory which also accounts for the way in which the hereditary causes work, we shall be able to produce a more satisfactory picture of the whole complex of causes which produce criminal behaviour in our modern world. (1977: 79)

Implicit in both bio-social and bio-psychological perspectives is the assumption that bad families, through a combination of biology and socialization, produce bad offspring: it is assumed that lower-class families impart more unconventional values to children who show a greater propensity for deviant acts. As Taylor, Walton, and Young suggest, psychogenic approaches to criminal behaviour lead to conclusions that

> The middle class, because of their use of 'love withdrawal' rather than 'primitive' techniques of child-rearing and because they base their moral discipline on well-defined principles, are superior to the working class in the quality of conditioning that they impart to their children. (1973: 62)

An overwhelming current of family indictment has persisted into more contemporary sociological explanations of criminal behaviour.

Given the persistence of psychological explanations for unconventional behaviour and the long-standing structural-functionalist tradition in criminology and family sociology, it is not surprising that the juvenile justice system, in its original form, was predicated on a system of scrutiny and restriction rather than on rehabilitation—although this contention is certainly arguable. The following section discusses, from a critical perspective, the history of juvenile justice in western societies, and reveals several phenomena which seem to illustrate the predominant conservative ideology regarding juvenile misbehaviour.

Critical Theory and the History of Juvenile Justice

Prior to the nineteenth century, few legal distinctions were made between juveniles and adults. Historically pre-modern, pre-nineteenth-century society did not acknowledge adolescence as a stage in human development. As Ariès suggests, the family in pre-industrial life, especially the lower-class family, was much more community-centred than the modern family. As a consequence, childhood autonomy and independence fostered a rapid transformation from childhood to adult responsibility: 'lower class children were mixed with adults. . . . They immediately went straight into the great community of men, sharing in the work and play of their companions, old and young alike' (1962: 411). Ariès describes a rather optimistic, idyllic view of pre-industrial childhood and extends his historical interpretation into a decidedly Marxist-based indictment of the rise of the private 'paterfamilias'. Private families, in concert with state institutions, came to insist on uniformity of conduct for adolescents and the scrutiny of such conduct through education. Donzelot echoes critical sentiments similar to those of Ariès when he places the rise of familism and the establishment of a system of juvenile scrutiny in the context of political power and control:

> The family constituted a clear dividing line between the defenders of the established order and those who contested it, between the capitalist camp and the socialist camp . . . conservatives who favoured the restoration of an established order

centering around the family, a return to an idealized former regime; but also liberals who saw the family as the protector of private property, of the bourgeois ethic of accumulation, as well as the guarantor of a barrier against the encroachments of the state. (1979: 5)

The political collision between right and left resulted in a moral movement fostered by an alliance between upper-class lobbyists and doctors. While there is considerable debate whether the efforts of these 'moral entrepreneurs' were based on humanitarian or self-serving motives, legislation like Canada's Juvenile Delinquency Act of 1908 tended to isolate and expose working-class families to increased surveillance and punishment. 'Government through families' was implemented by a 'tutelary complex' consisting of social work, education, medicine, religion, and juvenile courts. For Donzelot, the juvenile court had an insidious agenda directed at unconventional working-class families which were, in the Malthusian tradition, assumed to be sexually and morally bereft. He describes the juvenile court as one

> where the mode of appearance before the court implies the placing of the child and his family in a setting of notables, social technicians, and magistrates: an image of encirclement through the establishment of a direct communication between social imperatives and family behaviour, ratifying a relationship of force prejudicial to the family. (1979: 3)

Contemporary critical theorists like Foucault (1979) and Barrett and McIntosh (1982) argue that the nuclear family is constituted and supported to aid in capitalist production. The state responds to the demands of capitalism by helping to create and maintain the nuclear family as the legitimate family system in which the discipline necessary to be efficient in a productive society can be taught and monitored. The mechanisms which maintain and support the nuclear family as a device of social control include medicine, education, and the law. The family system, therefore, argue Barrett and McIntosh, is artificially— not naturally—created. Foucault describes the creation of the young as legal subjects or legal property in the context of familial power relations and disciplinary techniques. In his description of the children's prison at Mettray in France in 1840, Foucault suggests that a family/religion-based model of discipline and punishment was essential to the management of delinquent children and to the production of compliant and productive individuals. This model, he argues, has become the model of disciplinary techniques in modern institutions of social control:

> The chiefs and their deputies at Mettray had to be not exactly judges, or teachers, or foremen, or non-commissioned officer, or 'parents', but something of all these things in a quite specific mode of intervention. They were in a sense technicians of behaviour: engineers of conduct, orthopedists of individuality. Their task was to produce bodies that were both docile and capable. . . . The modelling of the body produces a knowledge of the individual, the apprenticeship of the techniques induces modes of behaviour, and the acquisition of skills is inextricably linked with the establishment of power relations; strong, skilled agricultural workers are

produced; in this very work, provided it is technically supervised, submissive subjects are produced and a dependable body of knowledge built up about them. (1979: 294-5)

R.D. Laing (1983) further supports the notion of the artificiality of the nuclear family unit. His thesis is that such a family unit is dialectic in nature, and that it is consequently fraught with contradictions and constraints on freedom. For Laing, as for Barrett and McIntosh, the family is essentially a political construct, characterized by two-parent homes and female subjugation and self-sacrifice, and predicated on the objective of class placement and political control. It is interesting to note the conspiratorial nature accorded to educational institutions in these historical analyses. Ariès concludes his research by suggesting that

Traditional apprenticeship was replaced by the school, an instrument of strict discipline, protected by the law-courts and the police courts. . . . The school shut a childhood which had hitherto been free within an increasingly severe disciplinary system, which culminated in the eighteenth and nineteenth centuries in the total claustration of the boarding-school. (1962: 413)

West (1984), in his historical analysis of Canadian education, further illustrates the rather insidious nature of education for marginalized children:

The school thus offered an institution whereby the state could control and exercise surveillance over not just all children, but almost all families in addition. The state could thus take an active part in helping to construct or promote those adult-child and family relations it deemed appropriate, while undermining others; it could shape the next generation's homes. (1984: 28)

The historical interest in education and its purported influence on adolescent conduct ironically parallels the theoretical arguments posed in the consensus theories of juvenile delinquency. Incompatibilities between education and the needs of certain individuals are seen as largely responsible for the creation of alienated, and ultimately delinquent, lower-class youth (Hirschi 1969; Hindelang 1973). However, for the critical theorists, elements of the social structure, like education, are unwilling or unable to address the needs of marginal children. Consensus theorists, on the other hand, focus on the failure of the child and the family to conform to the norms of the society.

Some critical theorists would allow that the initial motivation to create a juvenile justice system might have been based on generally humanitarian and philanthropic concerns. This benevolence was a response to the exploitation of children that became commonplace with the Industrial Revolution. (This exploitation and the ensuing criminality of youth is described in detail in Chapter Two.) The generally enlightened philosophy which grew in response to new industrialism made such exploitation a social problem. The 'Child Saving Movement' (Platt 1969), which presumably grew out of a deep social concern for child welfare, was based on the principle of *parens patriae*—the state was the ultimate guardian of the child. The Juvenile Delinquency Act of 1908 in

Canada, for example, gave the state, through the bureaucracy of the probation system, absolute authority to intervene forcibly in family life, abrogating the family's right to due process. Under the moral entrepreneurship of J.J. Kelso—a reporter and self-styled advocate for underprivileged children—the newly created juvenile justice system was given legal jurisdiction over families in the control of adolescents. Blame for unconventional activities was placed squarely on the shoulders of families, and causal explanations were premised on such ambiguous concerns as defective intelligence, uncaring parents, and poor home environments. Vague premises for state intervention eventually led to a juvenile justice bureaucracy which determined delinquency on the basis of such nebulous definitions as truancy, immoral behaviour, and incorrigibility, definitions which served to provide the system with a wide range of discretionary power. Advocates of *parens patriae* persisted well into the 1960s. They refused to accept juvenile delinquent actions as rationally motivated, and consequently professed a welfare rather than a legal approach to the treatment of children involved in crime. Eventually, the Civil Rights Movement, coupled with the whole social reform era of the 1960s, gradually led to a reform of the juvenile system, the early stages of which have now been determined by the Young Offenders Act in Canada, passed by Parliament in 1982. It was pre-dated by the Gault Decision of 1967 in the United States.

Philippe Meyer (1977) in *The Child and the State: The Intervention of the State in Family Life* discusses the history of the juvenile justice system in France and draws some rather critical conclusions regarding juvenile justice and its link to industrialism. The juvenile system described by Meyer was built on the same premises as those of North American justice with the same types of causal explanations involving defective mentalities, psychological disturbances, and blameworthy home environments. French civil law officially declared the family to be the fundamental unit of society and maintained that scrutiny of the family was a state priority. In the tradition of structural-functionalism, the French state defined the functional or 'regular' marriage on the basis of the typical nuclear family unit in which domesticity for women, moderation in family mores, and stable employment for men were the norms. Meyer's explanations for the existence of such a system of family law involve the state's need to maintain an economically functional family unit and to police activities which run contrary to the demands of capitalism. In essence, family law reflects the desire to reify the principles of economic production, to reproduce the relations of production, and to divorce the entrepreneurial classes from the labouring classes. Similar explanations for the North American juvenile system can be found in Platt (1969) for the United States, and in Hagan and Leon (1977) for Canada.

Platt's analysis of the history of American delinquency (1969) traces the formation of the juvenile court system in the United States and presents historical information similar to that in Meyer's analysis of France's juvenile justice system. Platt portrays the 'Child Saving Movement' in America as a middle-class, Anglo-Saxon, Protestant movement dedicated primarily to the control and the labelling of Catholic immigrant families. With the financial and moral support of the upper classes, religious bias, racism, and class discrimination culminated in the establishment of juvenile delinquency statutes throughout the states. These acts, which according to Platt expanded the power of the state over youth by inventing new categories of juvenile deviance, resulted in increasing rates of juvenile detention. To facilitate this, 'juvenile court functionaries were given the power to reach more juveniles and to commit them in increasing numbers to penal institutions' (1969: 173). The victims of the newly created professional bureaucracy were primarily the urban poor; as Platt suggests, 'the invention of delinquency consolidated the inferior social status and dependency of lower-class youth' (1969: 177).

Hagan and Leon (1977) argue that Platt's Marxist analysis of juvenile justice is unfounded, especially in relation to the 'Child Saving Movement' in Canada. The Canadian Juvenile Delinquency Act of 1908 gave juvenile authorities virtually unbridled discretionary power in the informal policing of juvenile conduct. Hagan and Leon suggest, however, that the legislation neither originated with industrial capitalistic concerns nor fostered the development of a specialized labour market characterized by renewed discipline and a renewed work ethic. The emphasis on probation as opposed to institutionalization or incarceration, they say, had generally admirable results: 'the overall effect was not to intensify a formal and explicit system of coercion, but rather to reinforce and increasingly intervene in informal systems of social control, particularly the family' (1977: 19). While Hagan and Leon's conclusions argue for a re-evaluation of the role of class conflict in the development of North American juvenile justice, it is nonetheless important that formal and informal intervention into family life implies wide discretionary power, power that has a distinct class bias especially in relation to the administration of juvenile justice in Canada.

How critical theorists interpret the historical underpinnings of juvenile delinquency and juvenile justice serves as background to Chapter Four's discussion of conflict theory and explanations of juvenile crime. The conflict approach, in its concern with justice and social inequality, reflects the concerns of social historians such as Ariès, Donzelot, and Foucault, whose historical accounts document economic disparity and political influence as progenitors of contemporary juvenile justice. These historical analyses, as well as less Marxist-oriented accounts (Hagan and Leon 1977), reveal a process of juvenile justice that is largely characterized by discretion and informality. On the critical claims regarding the class-based nature of juvenile justice, it is the position of this text's theoretical argument that the juvenile justice system is created and administered on the basis of an ideology that is largely reflective of class concerns and ideological influence.

chapter two

History of Canadian Young Offenders

The previous chapter presented the major theoretical positions on youth crime and justice and discussed critical theorists' understanding of the social and economic disparities influencing youth crime. Part of the critical argument is that to fully understand the social nature of Canadian youth justice requires an analysis of the history of the development of the society and the place of children within it. This history is characterized by laws and prohibitions that changed according to forces both economic and political. Government policy continually constructed and described the problems of juvenile delinquency as problems of class, gender, and ethnicity/immigration. I argue that the history of young offenders in Canada is a social rather than a legal history and that it chronicles the persistent prejudices and social-Darwinist beliefs of a powerful segment of Canadian society.

Immigration and Exploitation

This history effectively begins with pioneer society and the European settlement of Canada. Children in sixteenth- and seventeenth-century Canada were a considerable asset in subsistence-based communities and were protected and indulged. Their station changed with the immigration of indentured servants from England and France starting in the late seventeenth century. Well into the nineteenth century young girls and boys from the margins of European society were imported into Canada. They worked as indentured servants for Canada's bourgeoisie and as free labour for Canada's expanding industrial sector involving agricultural settlement, the fur trade, and westward exploration. Because these children were parentless and were considered to be from questionable backgrounds, they were blamed and punished for much of the youth misconduct of the time. As Carrigan's historical argument suggests, however, many of the crimes of youth were the direct result of exploitation:

> Many indentured servants were juvenile girls who were subject to the sexual exploitation that sometimes marked such a work arrangement. A servant who became pregnant was under a great deal of pressure to conceal her condition. Also, the chances for any young girl to find a desirable husband were substantially diminished if it became known that she had sexual relations. Consequently, young girls probably resorted to abortion and infanticide on occasion, as did their older sisters. To whatever extent they did, they were breaking the law of their day. (1991: 203)

At this point in history we first see evidence that Canada's youth justice policy had a decidedly exploitative side, and that judicial practice was, as a consequence, closely tied to the industrial needs of the society and to the social-Darwinist ideologies of wealthy and influential Canadians. Immigration of youths and the legal proscription of youth activity appears to have had a dual purpose: to facilitate economic expansion through indentured child labour; and to label and stigmatize the working and marginal classes as inferior and criminogenic. In addition, the socio-economic context of the time was characterized by major social changes which helped influence society's responses to young children. Rapid urbanization which accompanied the shift from agrarian to industrial society and the corresponding rise of the nuclear family which facilitated occupational mobility meant that traditional kinship ties were weakened. Contemporary belief held that human behaviour was influenced by environment and the family was the primary mechanism by which children were moulded. As Donzelot (1979) and Ariès (1962) argue, the concept of childhood and adolescent emerged at this time; children came to be viewed as distinct from adults. The family became the focus of social control efforts (Donzelot 1979), and the rise of the scientific method, which was the foundation of the development of positivism, resulted in medical, social, and political views that concentrated on children at risk. Such children were identified by certain social characteristics. As a result, intervention and rehabilitation became the mechanism of control and the reformatory became the site for that control (Griffiths and Verdun-Jones 1989).

It is important to understand that at this point in Canada's history, prevention dominated youth crime policy; children could be detained and incarcerated for their *potential* criminality. The idealistic argument that guided the institutionalization of youth at risk—and which guided the institutionalization movements of the eighteenth, nineteenth, and early twentieth centuries in general— was that institutions like reformatories exposed children to micro-societies that were more functional and productive than their families. In an era of the detection of potential delinquency, it is quite clear that illiteracy, cultural practices, and both moral and physical hygiene were viewed by those in power as causally related to delinquency. The social control machine rapidly expanded to include pre-delinquents, but the mechanisms for such control, including the reformatory and later the industrial school, were based ostensibly on philanthropic practices. However, the children who were caught and labelled were generally those from the margins of the society.

Later on in the nineteenth century, refugees from the famine in Ireland and orphans from poverty-ravaged Britain were received by Canada. Between 1873 and 1903, over 95,000 children came from Britain's slums and orphanages under the sponsorship of child immigration agencies (Carrigan 1991). Once again, the demand for these children was high because they served as domestic servants and field workers. And, once again, the beliefs held by wealthy Canadians created an atmosphere in which delinquency was equated with being an immigrant and being homeless. The term 'street arab' came to be attached to homeless juveniles who lived in overcrowded urban areas and who were uneducated, without parents, or unsupervised. Although only a small percentage of inmates in jail were juveniles, many 'street urchins' ended up in Kingston Penitentiary amongst the ranks of adult criminals.

The Socio-economic Nature of Youth Crime

As is the case with most youth crime of today, much of the juvenile crime in nineteenth-century Canada was minor, involving trespass, petty theft, and truancy. These types of criminal activity are now and long have been common amongst young people. Nevertheless, truancy came to be viewed as a detectable criminal trait amongst certain types of youth. While education was not compulsory at this time in Canada, children who were not in school were targeted as 'on the street' and much of the policing of youths was the result of a social welfare/custodial approach to truant and wayward youths. In much the same way that youth are arrested, detained, and punished today, Victorian youths were incarcerated not for the seriousness of the crime but rather because they were believed to be from unstable families. Children of respectable parents were much more immune to legal sanction for delinquent conduct. The following passage illustrates the ever-present relationship between wealth/respectability and justice:

> A school official preparing a report on delinquency in 1895 was surprised to find that a large number of problem children came 'from the homes of respectable, intelligent and well-to-do parents'. His discovery was based on his own study of young people rather than on arrest statistics. His findings once again suggest that delinquents from advantaged backgrounds were better able to cover up their offences. (Carrigan 1991: 214)

In addition to social class, geographical area helped determine legal privilege in nineteenth-century Canada. Urban youths who lived at the centre of the nineteenth-century city were much more likely to be caught by the law than were rural youths. The high visibility of urban youths and the concentration of policing efforts in inner-city urban areas contributed largely to an overrepresentation of central core urban juveniles in the justice system. Today, we find similar policing concentration in inner cities and in rural areas with high concentrations of police—typically Native reserve areas. The vulnerability of youths in these areas is amplified by their racial visibility and by the public nature of their activities.

Another bias evident in the history of Canadian juvenile delinquency control was the more severe intervention of the courts for female than for male offenders (Geller 1987; Chunn 1990). Gender-based differential treatment of offenders is a feature of our justice system to this day; courts tend to react more paternalistically (and protectively) to female young offenders. Carrigan (1991) points out that young female offenders at the turn of the century were often taken into custody for 'their own good'. Both social welfare agencies and the courts used the law to hold girls as young as four years old in closed custody. While many of these girls were the victims of neglect and were dealt with as such, those convicted of criminal offences were often initially arrested for minor infractions, the most common of these infractions being moral offences. Quite clearly, the initial criminal label that many girls experienced was the result of their familial, economic, and social situations. The law, as a result, translated privation into criminality and, ultimately, victim into offender. In this book, I argue that when agencies of social control detect, process, and punish certain categories of young offenders more so than others, they contribute not only to a double victimization, but also to the process of becoming a chronic offender (see the discussions on labelling theory in Chapter Four).

Youth Gangs and Crime Panics

Another historical dimension of Canadian youth crime which is often overlooked in spite of its applicability to the present is the perceived connection between drugs, gang violence, and youth crime. Carrigan (1991) argues that the growth of immigrant neighbourhoods in major Canadian cities in the first decades of the twentieth century resulted in the rise of youth gangs. His explanation is that immigrant youths, suffering discrimination and intimidation from the non-immigrant majority, formed gangs to provide security and social and economic opportunity. Political officials perceived the rise in juvenile crime in early twentieth-century Canada as the result of immigrant gangs being involved in inter-racial violence and drug trafficking and use. Carrigan points out that the perception of linkage between drug use and juvenile delinquency reached a point at which, in Vancouver, the justice system was asked to investigate the drug usage of all teenagers brought before the courts. The ensuing crime panic presented the picture of young persons being drawn into the dark web of criminal exploitation:

Newspapers carried stories claiming that young girls were being lured into prostitution through drugs and that young boys were selling in the streets. Dope dealers, it was claimed, were offering free drugs to young people to get them addicted. (Carrigan 1991: 221)

As it is today, however, it is difficult to determine the degree to which young people were engaged in the drug trade in the early decades of this century in Canada. More important, however, is the connection that was made by legal and political officials between race, immorality, and drugs at this time. Canadian social historians such as Melvyn Green (1986) and Elizabeth Comack (1991) trace the history of narcotics legislation in Canada, and argue that *The Opium and Drug Act* of 1911 was not a response to a real crime wave. On the contrary, the act was legislated through the efforts of politically influential people like Mackenzie King and Emily Murphy to stigmatize, for varying reasons, certain racial minorities. Green (1986) contends that powerful people like Judge Emily Murphy were influential in using legal norms to create a public morality transforming a private indulgence into a public crime. Murphy's *The Black Candle* (1922) is a scathing and unapologetic attack on racial minorities and the perceived immorality that determined their alleged drug abuse. The exposure and the credibility that this document received is evidenced by the fact that *Maclean's* magazine carried excerpts from the book for a period covering five issues. The sentiments of the documents were unabashed:

> It is claimed also, but with what truth we cannot say, that there is a well-defined propaganda among the aliens of color to bring about the degeneration of the white race. . . . It is hardly credible that the average Chinese peddler has any definite idea in his mind of bringing the downfall of the white race, his swaying motive being probably that of greed, but in the hands of his superiors, he may prove a powerful instrument to this very end. . . . whatever their motive, the traffic always comes with the Oriental, and . . . one would, therefore, be justified in assuming that it was their desire to injure the bright-browed races of the world. . . . Some of the Negroes coming into Canada . . . have similar ideas, and one of their greatest writers has boasted how, ultimately, they will control the white man. (Murphy 1922: 186-9)

Green (1986) maintains that the racist belief system (embedded in the previous passage) of a few powerful people was the driving force behind the legal prohibition of certain drugs such as opium in Canada, and that such legislation explicitly equated being evil with being foreign.

Given the fact that opium use had been a 'normal' activity in Canadian society for decades prior to 1908—even in the form of children's cough syrup—it is conceivable that forces other than merely crime control or racism were at work in the legislation of a new drug morality. Comack (1991) contends that the Anti-Opium Act of 1908 was, in essence, an attempt by politicians and industrialists to manage an economic crisis. From Comack's perspective, the alarm that was created over opium use and the ensuing drug legislation was mostly an attempt to pacify discontented labour by scapegoating minorities for the ills of the society. The crisis of labour, evidenced by growing class conflict—the result of capitalist activity—was redefined as a crisis of crime and immorality and served to manage the volatility of labour unions by directing public venom at immigrants.

There appears to be a clear and inescapable connection between legislation aimed at the 'immoral' habit practised by the Chinese and the ideology that an 'alien element' was responsible for the deteriorating situation in British Columbia. Opium-smoking became an easy symbol for the dangers and evils embodied in the fantasy of the 'Yellow Peril', and the opium legislation helped to affirm Oriental immigrants as a major cause of social problems.... In doing this, the law delegitimized further the competing view of the socialist movement, which insisted on defining labour issues in class, not racial terms. Moreover, the continuing identification of unrest with aliens was more-or-less a symbolic concession to the 'legitimate' conservative unions, which were willing to cooperate with capital (as contrasted with the so-called 'illegitimate' socialist unions that were more hostile to capital). In this fashion, the drug legislation drove another wedge, however small, into working class unity. (Comack 1991: 67)

Whether the drug panics of the early 1900s in Canada were the result of powerful moral agents or the collusion between government and business to control working peoples, it is quite clear that working-class immigrants were the primary targets of state intervention. It is more likely that the alarm over increasing drug usage by youths was the result of concerted political and media campaigns against specific marginal youths envisioned to be members of gangs, than that drug use was increasing amongst youth. Newspaper reports were preoccupied with young boys selling drugs and young girls being lured into prostitution through drugs (Carrigan 1991). The connections between moral degeneracy and drug use that occurred in media campaigns fostered by Murphy's *Black Candle* also occurred in public discourse surrounding youth deviance. Undoubtedly juveniles of the time did engage in drug use, but the political message was that moral degeneracy and drug use were primarily conditions of immigrants and marginal peoples, despite evidence, for example, that opium and heroin use occurred amongst professional groups like doctors.

The historical evidence suggests that in the period following the drug panics of the 1900s and the 1910s, youth crime was not restricted to the disadvantaged. Contrary to the perceptions of influential legislators, many law-breaking juveniles came from stable, conventional homes (Carrigan 1991). Given the evidence that the agencies of social control were directed primarily against 'street arabs', it is interesting that many advantaged youths ended up in youth detention. We might surmise that the courts, in response to the alarmist sentiments of politicians and the media, became rather more aggressive in prosecuting and sentencing youths; the widening net of youth control captured at least some of the advantaged youth who broke the law. Notwithstanding the newly realized involvement of privileged youths in criminal misconduct, the over-representation of lower-class youths in criminal statistics persisted into the middle decades of the twentieth century. The Department of Justice Committee on Juvenile Delinquency (1965) reported that children from families in the lower socio-economic levels of the society were over-represented in delinquency statistics, with the important and seemingly well-accepted caveat that privileged, middle-class offenders were dealt with through social agencies or parental surveillance rather than through legal channels.

In the modern era, we see public policy and commonsense perceptions of youth crime that are markedly similar to those of the past. Contemporary crime panics, especially those attacking the Young Offenders Act as too lenient, are once again based on perceptions of youth 'on the street'. And, as in the past, these public perceptions are based primarily on assessments of youth gangs as increasingly dangerous and increasingly foreign. The connections between race/ethnicity and youth appear to have persisted. Carrigan (1991), for example, discusses the current nihilistic behaviour of ethnically-based youth gangs, and suggests that amoral behaviour is common amongst juvenile delinquents and that modern-day youth deviants are peculiarly callous:

> Although the young have always been involved in violent and callous acts, such incidents were relatively rare in an earlier day. By the 1980s they had become much more common. In addition, there was growing evidence that violent young offenders were indifferent to the immorality of their actions and insensitive to the pain and suffering they were causing. Contemporary society faces a new kind of delinquent, some of whom portray an image of being basically amoral, undisciplined, societal outlaws, and oftentimes rootless. (Carrigan 1991: 231)

Furthermore, in public policy research the conviction predominates that certain ethnic groups are especially prone to violent and anti-social behaviour. Carrigan (1991) and Fowler (1993) report, for example, that not only are youth gangs becoming increasingly common in Canada's major cities, but that they are drawn from Latin America or specific countries like China or Viet Nam. The underlying message in much of the social analysis is that with immigration comes violence-prone youth.

> In recent years the Chinese gangs have stepped up their drug trafficking and extortion activities. The influx of immigrants has provided fresh recruits as well as better contacts in the East for drug supplies. Also, the large number of students who come to Canada from Hong Kong to study has created an expanding market for extortion. The gangs contact the parents of some of these students and demand protection money. While the Chinese have been the dominant Asian gangs for some time they are now being challenged by other ethnic groups.
>
> The flood of immigrants has brought with it some violence-prone youth from Latin American and from Vietnam and other Pacific countries. A typical example is the Vancouver-based Los Diablos, made up mostly of young people from Latin America and the Philippines. They started out as musclemen and law enforcers for the Chinese gangs but eventually struck out on their own and challenged their former employers for a share of the illegal business. Gang wars, brawls, and shootouts have resulted from the growing competition among these various ethnic gangs. Police have estimated that there are between 250 and 300 gang members active in Asian, Hispanic, and multi-ethnic gangs. (Carrigan 1991: 235-6)

I am not going to challenge the validity of the foregoing claims by social analysts. Certainly the phenomena of gang affiliation and youth violence are a concern to any modern system of crime control and justice. I would like to suggest, however, that these claims sound remarkably similar to those made about 'street arabs' around the turn of the century in Canada. Terms like 'flood of immigrants' conjure up images of youth violence and crime somehow inextricably tied to immigration and ethnicity. What is important, in addition, is that the crime panics and the ensuing public policy changes result from perceptions of only certain youths as potential criminals. These perceptions, I argue, colour the sentiments and attitudes not only of mainstream society, but also of those who are in a position to pass judgement on violators.

In the following chapter I present an empirical description of official juvenile crime in Canada. Because the data are based on official statistics, they do not necessarily indicate changes in actual crime committed (although they may do so in part); rather, the historical and contemporary trends depicted in Chapter Three primarily reveal changes in policing and judicial policy over time, especially with respect to the Young Offenders Act.

Historical and Contemporary Trends in Official Juvenile Crime Rates

The legal definition of youth crime has historically depended on the ideologies of influential segments of the society. As a result, the numbers and types of children who have been caught in the web of control have been the result of changing political and economic forces. In addition, evidence suggests that delinquent behaviour is universal, and most youth misconduct is inconsequential and fleeting. That is an important consideration in assessing the following data on youth crime rates. This chapter offers both historical and contemporary documentation on youth crime rates in Canada.

Canadian Youth Crime Rates Over Time

Historical trends in official youth crime statistics illustrate that the numbers of youth crimes detected and processed informally and formally have varied dramatically, especially since the legislation of the Young Offenders Act in 1984. I maintain that official rates of youth crime are not necessarily related to crime committed, but rather to certain historical phenomena such as law reform. I make no attempt here to test the causal origins of youth crime. I posit, however, that the marked fluctuations in crime rates are largely indicative of the changing political nature of crime control, and not simply a result of increased criminal activity of youth.

Trends in Formal and Informal Handling

Figure 1 presents the historical trends in official rates of criminal code violations: total violations, violations handled formally, and violations handled

Figure 1: Criminal Code Offences—total, informally, and formally handled

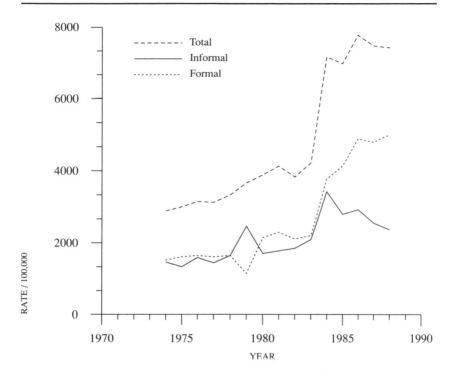

informally. Formal cases are handled through the courts where the accused is required to enter a plea and have his or her case adjudicated through legal process. Informal cases are handled outside of the legal process at the discretion of the police and court officials—the police detain a young offender and, rather than lay a charge, release the child to its parents or to child welfare agencies. These cases, which do not require legal process and are handled through informal agreements between juridical officials, the youth, and the parents or guardians, accord with the underlying philosophy of the Young Offenders Act.

Figure 1 shows the overall trends in the nature of legal processing of young offenders for all criminal code violations.

The most noticeable aspect of Figure 1 is the substantial increase in all categories after the implementation of the Young Offenders Act in 1984. Total cases increased in number from 1983 to 1986 and then levelled off. However, cases handled informally increased in number from 1983 to 1984 and then dropped off somewhat. At the same time, cases handled formally increased sharply from 1983 and continued to increase although less swiftly. Much of the initial rapid increase in total cases can be explained by the fact that youth courts, since the Young Offenders Act, have processed seventeen- and eighteen-year-olds, where these youth were previously handled in adult court. This does

Figure 2: Violent Offences—total, informally, and formally handled

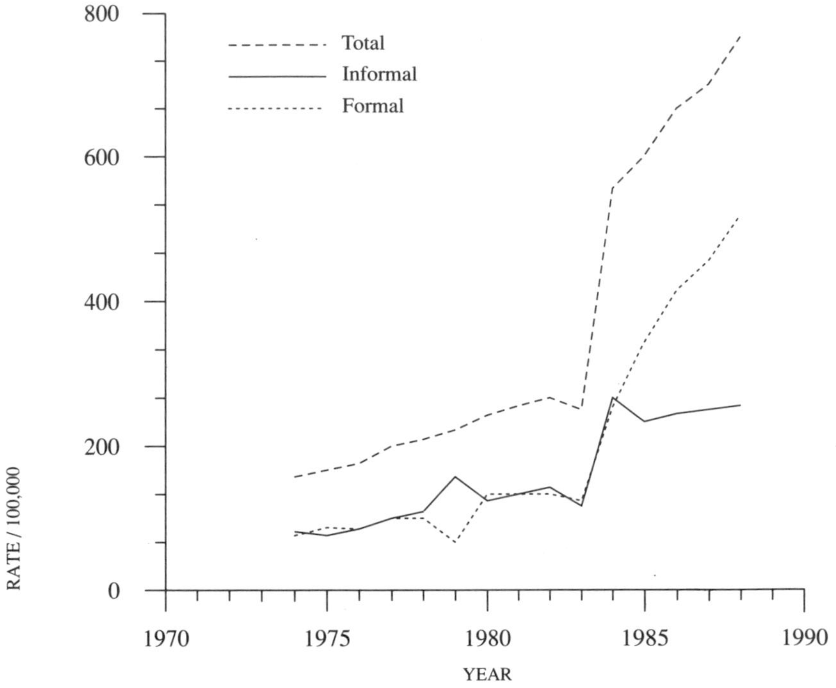

not explain, however, why the rapid upward trend continued for several years before levelling off. Some of the increase may be the result of provincial jurisdictions experimenting with adjusting age guidelines in accordance with particular provincial and territorial needs.

Also, in light of the philosophy of the Young Offenders Act to encourage and use diversion and alternative measures as much as possible, it is noteworthy that formal handling of cases continued to increase from 1984, the period when the number of cases handled informally started to decrease. Although I have reasoned previously that the increase in the number of cases may be the result of uncertainty surrounding the new Act, it is more difficult to explain why, in the spirit of diversion and informality, greater proportions of youth have been processed formally. We might surmise, however, that since the inception of Young Offenders Act, the police are much less hesitant to arrest knowing that young offenders will likely receive alternative measures rather than custodial dispositions.

Figures 2 and 3 show the official youth crime rates over time for the specific categories of violent and property crimes, respectively. It is here that we observe differences in processing of youth based on the type and seriousness of crime

Figure 3: Property Offences—total, informally, and formally handled

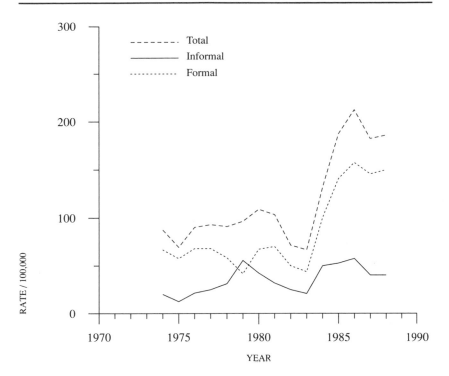

committed. Figure 2 illustrates that the trends for violent offences do not parallel those for overall criminal code violations.

Specifically, both total cases and cases handled formally increased in number dramatically for the initial period, as observed in Figure 1. However, the sharp increases appear to continue past the initial reaction period and up to 1988. At the same time, the number of cases handled informally increased coincidentally with the formal cases only for the period 1983-1984, at which point on the graph the two trend lines diverge dramatically. Quite clearly, youth courts have increasingly chosen formal legal procedures to deal with violent offences in contravention of the principles of diversion encompassed in the Young Offenders Act.

Figure 3 shows that youth courts handle property cases differently from violent offences.

Both total offences and offences handled formally increased in number rapidly from 1983 until 1986, at which point the trends reversed and fewer cases were handled by youth courts. Similar trends appeared for the number of cases handled informally with the qualification that the increases were much smaller and the levelling-off process occurred immediately (1984-1985). Overall, the trend lines in Figure 3 illustrate once again the tendency of youth courts to deal

Figure 4: Drug Offences—total, informally, and formally handled

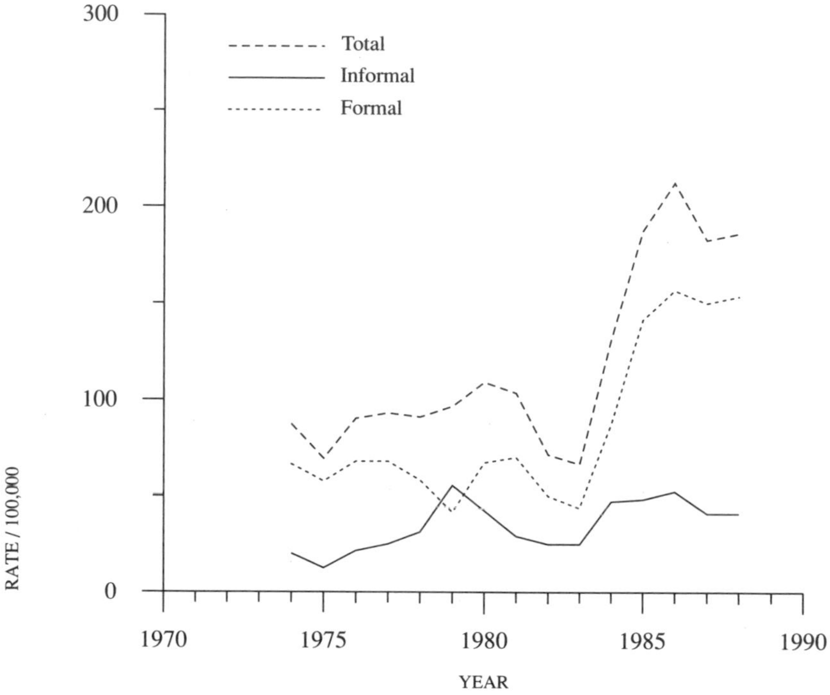

formally rather than informally with young offenders since the announcement of the Young Offenders Act in 1983.

Figures 4 and 5 present drug and alcohol violations respectively for the same time periods as described for violent and property offences. Figure 4 illustrates that both total drug offences and drug cases that were handled formally increased considerably after 1983.

The initial period after the Young Offenders Act saw increases in the numbers of both formal and informal cases. Subsequently, the number of cases handled informally levelled off while the number of formal cases increased until 1986. After 1986, both formal and informal cases decreased somewhat. As with the previous graphs, the initial adjustment in official crime rates attributable to the inclusion of seventeen- and eighteen-year-olds in a restructured youth justice system was followed by an increase in formal cases and a decrease in informal cases. It is interesting that against the spirit of alternative measures and diversion highlighted in the Young Offenders Act, the number of cases handled formally increased markedly after the initial adjustment year.

Moving from drug to liquor offences, we notice much the same types of fluctuations.

The most significant difference between drug and alcohol offences is the

Figure 5: Liquor Offences—total, informally, and formally handled

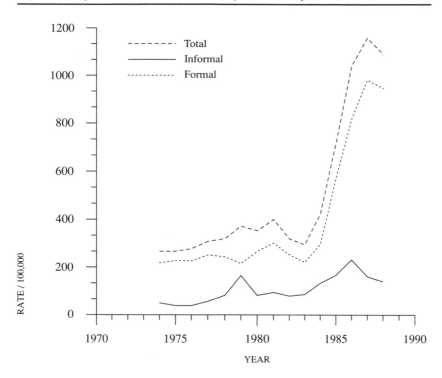

dramatic increase in total alcohol offences and alcohol offences handled formally from the inception of the Young Offenders Act to 1987. A slight levelling off occurred from 1987 to 1988 but overall, the youth justice system appears to have been inundated with liquor offences in the years subsequent to the Young Offenders Act. It is worth commenting that in the legal arena liquor offences are regarded as less serious than drug offences. We might expect, therefore, that liquor offences would tend to be handled relatively less formally than drug offences, especially after the Young Offenders Act. In fact, the opposite appears to be true, supporting claims that the Young Offenders Act may be more punitive than its predecessor.

Figure 6 illustrates the final category of offences, defined as 'other offences' — a catch-all category for minor offences including general violations of disturbing the peace, being unlawfully at large, trespassing, and mischief, among others.

As with the trends discussed in the previous five figures, a marked increase in offences occurred immediately after the implementation of the Young Offenders Act with a levelling off after 1986. Most noticeable for this category of offences, however, is that the majority of cases were handled informally up to 1986, at which time the proportion of formal cases surpassed that of the

Figure 6: Other Offences—total, informally, and formally handled

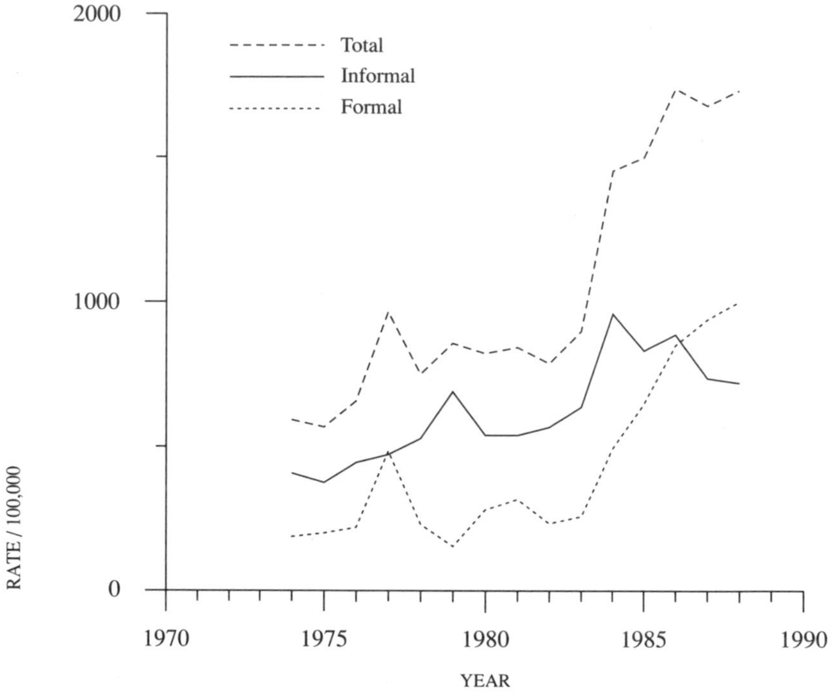

informal cases. And, again, although total cases levelled off after 1986, the number of formally processed cases increased in a linear fashion while the informal cases decreased in a similar manner. It is also noteworthy that prior to the Young Offenders Act, the ratio of informal to formal cases remained relatively high; with the exception of 1977, this ratio diminished only after the Young Offenders Act. The spirit of the Young Offenders Act seems to have been violated once again.

Trends in Male and Female Youth Charged

The preceding analysis suggests quite clearly that the Young Offenders Act has changed the nature and magnitude of youth justice. The increases in overall offences are attributable primarily to the inclusion of older youth in the Young Offenders Act. The increases after the initial correction, however, indicate that the magnitude of social control in the current youth system is greater than in its predecessor. Furthermore, this claim is accentuated by the increasing tendency towards formal procedures for all categories of offences.

The next series of figures illustrates the comparative historical changes in official crime rates for male and female young offenders. The line graphs are not

Figure 7: Total Criminal Code Offences—male and female

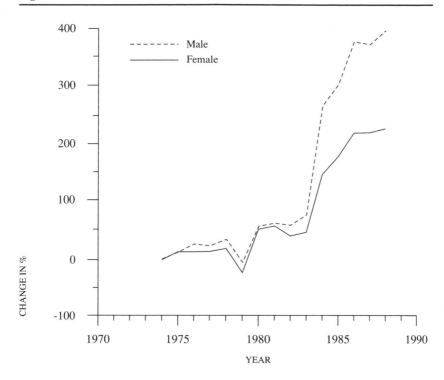

based on rates of crime, but rather on percentage changes in rates relative to the baseline year of 1974. The figures illustrate the changes that have taken place since 1974 for female and male youth, and they cover the offence categories discussed in the previous figures. Figure 7 presents total criminal code offences for male and female youth.

Interestingly, for the years preceding the Young Offenders Act, percentage changes in offence rates for male and female offenders were similar. In 1984, however, percentage changes in male rates increased more rapidly than female rates. Although a levelling did occur in 1986, increases in both male and female rates were still occurring after 1986. Line graphs for specific crime categories, however, indicate differential trends for males and females. Figures 8 and 9 show trends for violent and property offences.

The figures reveal that the trend regarding total criminal code offences is reversed with rates for female offenders increasing more rapidly than for male offenders. For violent offences, the gap between males and females becomes increasingly wide after the Young Offenders Act, and no levelling is observed. Up to the inception of the Young Offenders Act, the percentage change in violent crime rates is almost equal. For property offences, similar trends are apparent with female rates increasing more dramatically than male rates. Unlike

Figure 8: Violent Offences—male and female

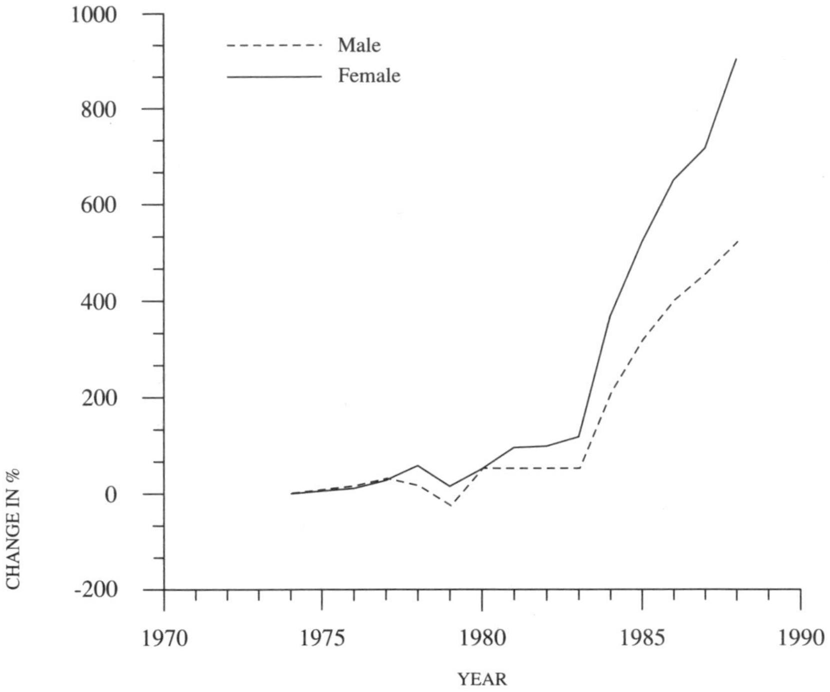

violent offences, however, a levelling in the trends occurs for both males and females beginning in 1986. It is clear that for property and violent offences, the youth justice system handled relatively more female than male offenders as of the implementation of the Young Offenders Act.

For drug and alcohol offences the trends are reversed.

For drug offences (see Figure 10) changes in male and female rates are quite similar with the exception of the last few years in which male rates have increased more than female rates. For alcohol offences (see Figure 11) the differences are more striking. From 1984 to 1987, male rates increased sharply, and although female rates increased as well, the increases were less dramatic than those for males. Interestingly, for both drug and alcohol offences prior to the Young Offenders Act, percentage increases in offence rates are strikingly similar.

Finally, with respect to the 'other offence' category, once again male and female offenders were treated similarly only until the implementation of the Young Offenders Act. For this category of relatively non-serious offences, after the Young Offenders Act, female rates increased more sharply than male rates, and for both, there was no levelling of trends. It is interesting that, given the non-serious nature of offences encompassed in this category, the extent of control experienced by youth has been much greater since the Young Offenders

Figure 9: Property Offences—male and female

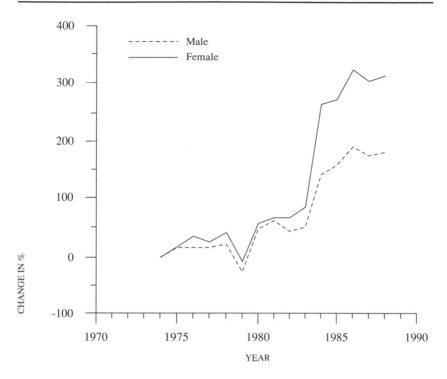

CHANGE IN %

YEAR

Act. The persistence of the increases up to 1988 for both males and females suggests that the increases after the Young Offenders Act were not entirely a function of the increased age categories covered under the act. We might surmise that given the increased non-custodial alternatives in the Young Offenders Act, police are more willing to arrest young offenders, especially non-serious female offenders.

While it is difficult to understand the nature of crime and justice based on official statistics, the data show quite clearly that trends in official crime rates have changed significantly since the announcement of the Young Offenders Act. Overall, the total number of cases handled have increased for all offences; this is partly the result of the inclusion of older youth in the new act. However, many of the increases in official rates of crime have been sustained since the initial adjustment period for age. Most significant has been the general rapid increase in the number of cases handled formally. Prior to the Young Offenders Act, for most offences the number of formal cases did not significantly outnumber the informal cases. Moreover, for non-serious offences, the informal cases actually were greater than the formal. I argue in the following chapter that in the context of the Young Offenders Act, the police may be more disposed to lay a charge given the increased 'mild' alternatives to custodial dispositions. Police

Figure 10: Drug Offences—male and female

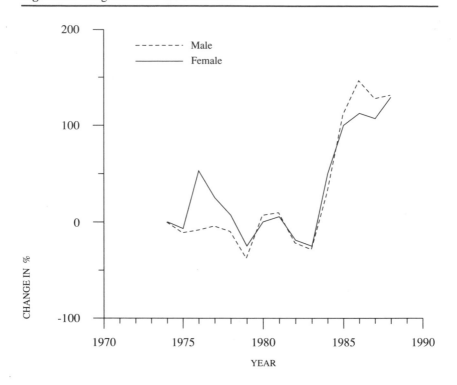

may believe that arrest and alternative measures are in the best interests of the young offender.

The same conclusions can be drawn from the trends for males and females. Based on the nature of the offence, males and females show differential changes in offence rates. For property, violent, and non-serious offences, female rates have increased more rapidly than male rates; although female rates are still considerably lower than male rates, some convergence occurs. The exception to general convergence appears in substance abuse. Especially for liquor offences, the percentage change in male rates is markedly higher than for female rates. The difference, however, is much smaller for drug offences. The widening gap between the number of males and females charged may be indicative of the widening gap in actual substance-abuse offences committed.

Current Trends in Youth Justice

While there are few actual data on the administration of youth courts in Canada, national data on the cases heard in youth courts and the outcomes of those cases give some indication of the nature, extent, and treatment of youth crime. We get no indication of the dark or hidden dimension of youth crime from these

Figure 11: Alcohol Offences—male and female

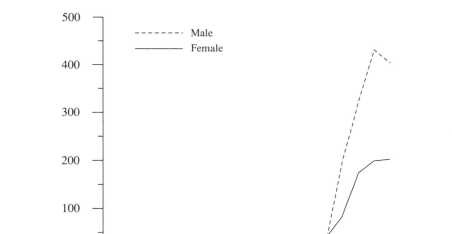

data, however, only a picture of the formal handling of youths who come to court. As I have argued previously in this book and will show in the following chapter, the official data on youth crime in Canada present a somewhat distorted picture of actual crime committed. Most importantly, these data tend to over-represent certain categories of youth. Nonetheless, we can see from the following tables that certain types of legal outcomes are more prevalent for certain youths, and that the courts use certain avenues of justice and control more than others.

Table 3.1 illustrates the numbers of cases heard by youth courts in Canada in 1991-92 in percentage by the age and sex of the accused.

For violent offences by males, the proportion of offences increases with age. For females, however, the greatest proportion of total offences occurs in the fifteen-year age group; the same phenomenon occurs for the specific violent offences of assault and robbery. For murder, there are so few cases from which to suggest tendencies exception that for males, the majority of cases are for seventeen-year-olds. The occurrences of sexual assault, however, present several unexpected trends. Firstly, the proportions in each age category are relatively even across the fourteen- to sixteen-year age groups with a lower proportion for

Figure 12: Other Offences—male and female

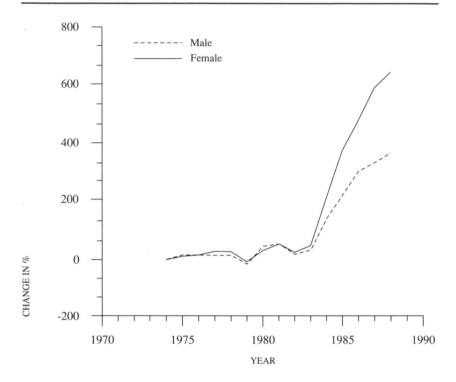

seventeen-year-olds. Secondly—and somewhat surprisingly—33 cases of sexual assault were committed by female offenders.

For property offences, the proportions of females and males within each age group reflect previous trends; the greatest number of offenders within each gender category are older males and fifteen-year-old females. The same phenomenon holds true for all the specific property offences with the exception of motor vehicle theft in which the ages are lower than for other property offences. For example, for females who commit car theft, the predominant ages are fourteen and fifteen, and for males fifteen and sixteen. For some reason, the older offenders tend to commit motor vehicle theft less often than do younger offenders, especially in relation to other property offences. This may be because younger offenders are not of legal driving age, so that it is virtually impossible to experience the thrill of driving without stealing a car. However, the vast majority of arrests for impaired operation occurs in the oldest category for males and females, evidence that they are of legal driving age and are much more likely to be caught in an impaired situation.

The last set of offences in this table is interesting because of the relatively low number of incidences of violations for charges like drug possession, trafficking, and narcotics offences. Such low rates are expected for murder/manslaughter,

Table 3.1 Cases Heard by Youth Courts in Canada by Principal Charge, Age and Sex of the Accused, 1991–92

PRINCIPAL CHARGE		TOTAL	AGE								
			<12	12	13	14	15	16	17	>17	UNKNOWN
TOTAL	T	116,397 (100%)	0.03%	2.84%	7.39%	14.30%	20.76%	25.04%	26.71%	1.44%	1.48%
	M	82.31%	0.03%	2.73%	6.90%	13.29%	20.11%	25.62%	28.32%	1.52%	1.48%
	F	17.69%	0.03%	3.37%	9.69%	19.03%	23.75%	22.37%	19.21%	1.06%	1.48%
VIOLENT OFFENCES	T	19,824 (100%)	0.04%	3.42%	8.14%	14.56%	20.85%	24.36%	26.07%	0.31%	2.25%
	M	82.11%	0.03%	3.37%	7.69%	13.34%	20.21%	24.98%	27.89%	0.32%	2.18%
	F	17.89%	0.06%	3.64%	10.18%	20.19%	23.82%	21.54%	17.73%	0.25%	2.59%
Murder/Manslaughter	T	51 (100%)	—	1.96%	1.96%	15.69%	19.61%	21.57%	37.25%	—	1.96%
	M	86.27%	—	2.27%	2.27%	2.27%	15.91%	20.45%	25.00%	—	2.27%
	F	13.73%	—	—	—	14.29%	14.29%	—	71.43%	—	—
Sexual Assault	T	1,639 (100%)	0.06%	7.44%	13.73%	19.10%	19.59%	19.52%	17.39%	1.46%	1.71%
	M	97.93%	0.06%	7.48%	13.58%	19.13%	19.63%	19.69%	17.38%	1.43%	1.62%
	F	2.07%	—	5.88%	20.59%	17.65%	17.65%	11.76%	17.65%	2.94%	5.88%
Assault	T	12,869 (100%)	0.02%	3.37%	8.36%	14.46%	21.24%	24.04%	26.09%	0.15%	2.28%
	M	76.34%	0.01%	3.21%	7.59%	12.70%	20.28%	24.90%	28.91%	0.12%	2.19%
	F	23.66%	0.03%	3.91%	10.54%	20.13%	24.33%	21.28%	16.98%	0.23%	2.56%

Table 3.1 (continued)

PRINCIPAL CHARGE		TOTAL	AGE								
			<12	12	13	14	15	16	17	>17	UNKNOWN
Robbery	T	2,209 (100%)	0.05%	2.13%	5.57%	13.54%	20.05%	27.98%	27.48%	0.27%	2.94%
	M	86.96%	0.05%	2.24%	5.62%	11.71%	19.73%	28.47%	28.94%	0.26%	2.97%
	F	13.04%	—	1.39%	5.21%	25.69%	22.22%	24.65%	17.71%	0.35%	2.78%
PROPERTY OFFENCES	T	66,724 (100%)	0.04%	3.41%	8.29%	15.63%	21.49%	25.18%	24.42%	0.24%	1.29%
	M	83.73%	0.05%	3.25%	7.81%	14.81%	21.06%	25.77%	25.69%	0.26%	1.30%
	F	16.27%	0.04%	4.22%	10.78%	19.85%	23.71%	22.12%	17.90%	0.13%	1.24%
Break and Enter	T	17,547 (100%)	0.05%	3.45%	8.00%	15.19%	21.18%	26.02%	24.61%	0.25%	1.25%
	M	93.62%	0.05%	3.29%	7.64%	14.76%	20.99%	26.41%	25.31%	0.25%	1.30%
	F	6.38%	—	5.81%	13.32%	21.54%	23.95%	20.38%	14.30%	0.18%	0.54%
Motor Vehicle Theft	T	1,609 (100%)	—	2.36%	7.77%	17.09%	26.85%	24.98%	19.64%	0.12%	1.18%
	M	83.78%	—	1.85%	7.49%	15.06%	26.41%	26.34%	21.59%	0.15%	1.11%
	F	16.22%	—	4.98%	9.20%	27.59%	29.12%	18.01%	9.58%	—	1.53%
Theft >$1,000	T	4,421 (100%)	—	1.63%	5.54%	13.50%	22.82%	27.35%	27.75%	0.18%	1.22%
	M	91.34%	—	1.49%	4.80%	12.65%	23.20%	27.81%	28.60%	0.20%	1.24%
	F	8.66%	—	3.13%	13.32%	22.25%	18.80%	22.45%	18.80%	—	1.04%

Table 3.1 (continued)

PRINCIPAL CHARGE	TOTAL	AGE								
		<12	12	13	14	15	16	17	>17	UNKNOWN
Theft <$1,000										
T	24,247 (100%)	0.03%	4.13%	10.12%	17.52%	21.73%	23.92%	21.19%	0.19%	1.15%
M	73.52%	0.03%	4.11%	9.62%	16.72%	21.01%	24.50%	22.65%	0.22%	1.13%
F	26.48%	0.03%	4.20%	11.51%	19.73%	23.75%	22.32%	17.16%	0.11%	1.18%
Possession of Stolen Property										
T	8,013 (100%)	0.05%	2.01%	5.33%	14.00%	21.98%	27.17%	27.64%	0.32%	1.50%
M	88.29%	0.06%	1.84%	4.93%	12.88%	21.63%	28.08%	28.75%	0.33%	1.51%
F	11.71%	—	3.30%	8.32%	22.49%	24.63%	20.26%	19.30%	0.32%	1.39%
OTHER CRIMINAL CODE										
T	18,165 (100%)	0.01%	1.51%	5.14%	11.07%	18.20%	26.26%	32.88%	3.45%	1.49%
M	78.85%	0.01%	1.34%	4.48%	9.80%	17.16%	26.81%	35.28%	3.56%	1.56%
F	21.15%	0.03%	2.13%	7.60%	15.78%	22.085	24.21%	23.90%	3.05%	1.22%
Impaired Operation										
T	1,264 (100%)	—	0.08%	0.08%	1.03%	5.06%	25.24%	68.04%	0.32%	0.16%
M	88.69%	—	0.09%	—	0.89%	4.73%	23.73%	70.03%	0.36%	0.18%
F	11.31%	—	—	0.70%	2.10%	7.69%	37.06%	52.45%	—	—
Unlawfully at Large/Failure to Appear										
T	10,577 (100%)	0.01%	1.70%	6.15%	12.50%	19.47%	25.05%	28.15%	5.50%	1.47%
M	77.04%	0.01%	1.51%	5.33%	10.80%	18.06%	25.86%	31.01%	5.82%	1.61%
F	22.96%	—	2.35%	8.90%	18.20%	24.18%	22.36%	18.53%	4.45%	1.03%

Table 3.1 (continued)

PRINCIPAL CHARGE	TOTAL	AGE								
		<12	12	13	14	15	16	17	>17	UNKNOWN
Soliciting										
T	359 (100%)	—	—	1.39%	5.57%	13.37%	30.64%	49.03%	—	—
M	8.63%	—	—	—	3.33%	10.00%	30.00%	56.67%	—	—
F	91.64%	—	—	1.52%	5.78%	13.78%	30.70%	48.33%	—	—
NARCOTIC CONTROL ACT										
T	2,077 (100%)	—	0.14%	1.30%	5.58%	15.12%	27.83%	47.76%	0.48%	1.78%
M	84.88%	—	0.06%	1.30%	5.16%	14.86%	27.06%	49.57%	0.23%	1.76%
F	15.12%	—	0.64%	1.27%	7.96%	16.56%	32.17%	37.58%	1.91%	1.91%
Trafficking in Narcotics										
T	674 (100%)	—	—	0.89%	6.38%	16.62%	30.86%	42.88%	0.74%	1.63%
M	86.05%	—	—	1.03%	6.72%	16.03%	30.00%	44.14%	0.34%	1.72%
F	13.95%	—	—	—	4.26%	20.21%	36.17%	35.11%	3.19%	1.06%
Possession of Narcotics										
T	1,378 (100%)	—	0.22%	1.52%	5.22%	14.30%	26.27%	50.44%	0.36%	1.67%
M	84.98%	—	0.09%	1.45%	4.36%	14.18%	25.53%	52.43%	0.17%	1.79%
F	15.02%	—	0.97%	1.93%	10.14%	14.98%	30.43%	39.13%	1.45%	0.97%
YOUNG OFFENDERS ACT										
T	9,138 (100%)	—	0.84%	5.32%	12.86%	21.67%	22.50%	26.77%	8.96%	1.08%
M	78.39%	—	0.74%	4.45%	10.65%	19.82%	23.17%	29.64%	10.43%	1.09%
F	21.61%	—	1.22%	8.46%	20.86%	28.35%	20.05%	16.35%	3.65%	1.06%
Failure to Comply with Disposition										
T	9,123	—	0.83%	5.32%	12.86%	21.67%	22.47%	26.80%	8.79%	1.09%
M	78.38%	—	0.73%	4.45%	10.64%	19.84%	23.13%	29.67%	10.45%	1.09%
F	21.62%	—	1.22%	8.47%	20.89%	28.30%	20.08%	16.38%	3.60%	1.06%

but seem amazingly low for drug charges. In addition, charges for soliciting, while relatively few in number, illustrate that soliciting is much more common amongst older offenders and, as expected, amongst females. However, the proportion of males to females is much smaller than the reported proportion of prostitutes in the population of Canada (the oft-quoted figure is one male to four female prostitutes (Special Committee on Pornography and Prostitution 1985). Arrest figures indicate that females are detected relatively more often for soliciting than males, proportionate to the actual number of young male and female prostitutes on the street. Finally, the charges for youth court violations, including being at large, failure to appear and comply, and YOA infractions illustrate the same trends for the majority of offences in this table; the predominant age category for males is seventeen and for females is fifteen.

Overall, it appears that for most crimes, male involvement increases steadily with an increase in age, while female involvement in crime is mostly curvilinear. That is, for females, criminal behaviour or the likelihood of being detected for criminal behaviour peaks at fifteen and then subsides. Although we might speculate that the majority of females cease unconventional activity and become so-called responsible citizens at an earlier age than do males. The conventional wisdom is that females mature generally two years earlier than males and the arrest rates may reflect this phenomenon. In this book I argue, however, that the crime rates are partly reflective of selective policing; given that youth misconduct is universal, it is plausible that females are dealt with more harshly than males at earlier ages. Specifically, the police tend to react more legalistically to young female offenders than to young male offenders, and such legal paternalism may be reflected in the gender disparities that we see for most offences in this table. This gender disparity has been mentioned often in research on youth crime and justice (Barnhorst 1980; Geller 1987, 1980; Campbell 1981).

Table 3.2 illustrates the number and percentage of cases heard by youth courts in Canada in 1991-92, and the most significant decision rendered in each case by the age and sex of the accused.

Most notable here is the large proportion of cases in which a guilty decision was reached (64.6 per cent). In addition, the proportion of cases where a not-guilty decision was reached is only 1.3 per cent, a statistic which indicates that the youth courts are not a place where the vast majority of youth either decide to plead not guilty or where their guilty pleas are successfully defended. The next largest category involves cases that are withdrawn (22.8 per cent); this figure is interesting in contrast to cases dismissed (4 per cent). The courts likely withdraw minor charges in many cases in which there are multiple offences committed, a procedure which simplifies the administration of the courts while maintaining the primary offence as the most serious offence.

Some of the contrasts across age categories and between categories of sex are noteworthy here. For example, in most categories of decision, females are most numerous in the fifteen-year-old age group, especially for the total and guilty categories. Correspondingly, males are most numerous primarily in the

Table 3.2 Cases Heard by Youth Courts in Canada, by Most Significant Decision, Age and Sex of the Accused, 1991–92

MOST SIGNIFICANT DECISION	TOTAL	AGE								
		<12	12	13	14	15	16	17	>17	UNKNOWN
TOTAL										
T	116,397 (100%)	0.03%	2.85%	7.39%	14.30%	20.75%	25.05%	26.72%	1.44%	1.48%
M	82.31%	0.03%	2.73%	6.89%	13.28%	20.11%	25.63%	28.33%	1.52%	1.48%
F	17.69%	0.03%	3.38%	9.69%	19.02%	23.76%	22.37%	19.21%	1.06%	1.48%
Transfer to Adult Court										
T	71 (100%)	—	—	—	1.41%	7.04%	18.31%	64.79%	8.45%	—
M	95.77%	—	—	—	1.47%	5.88%	17.65%	66.18%	8.82%	—
F	4.23%	—	—	—	—	33.33%	33.33%	33.33%	—	—
Guilty (64.6%)										
T	75,143 (100%)	0.02%	2.64%	7.28%	14.33%	21.13%	25.41%	27.29%	0.89%	1.00%
M	84.05%	0.01%	2.53%	6.81%	13.36%	20.59%	25.98%	28.82%	0.91%	0.99%
F	15.95%	0.01%	3.25%	9.76%	19.45%	24.03%	22.42%	19.25%	0.80%	1.03%
Not Guilty (1.3%)										
T	1,517 (100%)	—	2.90%	5.41%	11.47%	19.51%	26.76%	32.10%	0.72%	1.12%
M	87.01%	—	2.35%	5.30%	10.53%	19.62%	27.27%	33.18%	0.66%	1.06%
F	12.99%	—	6.60%	6.09%	17.77%	18.78%	23.35%	24.87%	1.02%	1.52%
Proceedings Stayed (9.1%)										
T	8,295 (100%)	0.06%	3.45%	7.53%	13.39%	19.46%	23.66%	26.15%	5.40%	0.89%
M	81.19%	0.06%	3.33%	7.07%	12.23%	18.74%	23.88%	27.82%	5.86%	1.01%
F	18.81%	0.06%	3.97%	9.55%	18.40%	22.56%	22.76%	18.91%	3.40%	0.38%

Table 3.2 (continued)

MOST SIGNIFICANT		AGE									
DECISION	TOTAL	<12	12	13	14	15	16	17	>17	UNKNOWN
Dismissed (4.08%)										
T	4,675 (100%)	0.06%	3.53%	7.83%	14.48%	20.73%	24.32%	26.40%	0.90%	1.75%
M	80.46%	0.03%	3.67%	7.42%	14.17%	19.91%	24.32%	27.72%	1.04%	1.73%
F	19.53%	0.22%	2.96%	9.53%	15.77%	24.10%	24.32%	20.92%	0.33%	1.86%
Withdrawn (22.8%)										
T	26,563 (100%)	0.06%	3.12%	7.59%	14.61%	20.17%	24.53%	24.93%	1.87%	3.02%
M	77.74%	0.06%	3.02%	7.11%	13.40%	19.19%	25.30%	26.69%	2.10%	3.13%
F	22.26%	0.05%	3.47%	9.74%	18.84%	23.61%	21.85%	18.76%	1.07%	2.60%
Transfer to other Jurisdiction										
T	87 (100%)	—	3.45%	1.15%	14.49%	18.39%	29.80%	29.89%	2.30%	—
M	88.51%	—	3.90%	1.30%	14.29%	15.58%	31.17%	31.17%	2.60%	—
F	11.49%	—	—	—	20.00%	40.00%	20.00%	20.00%	—	—
Other										
T	46 (100%)	—	—	13.04%	32.61%	36.96%	6.52%	8.70%	2.17%	—
M	73.91%	—	—	14.71%	29.41%	41.18%	8.82%	5.88%	—	—
F	26.09%	—	—	8.33%	41.67%	25.00%	—	16.67%	8.33%	—

Table 3.3 Cases Heard by Youth Courts in Canada, by Most Significant Disposition, Age, and Sex of the Accused, 1991–92

MOST SIGNIFICANT DISPOSITION	TOTAL	AGE								
		<12	12	13	14	15	16	17	>17	UNKNOWN
TOTAL (100%)										
T	75,143 (100%)	0.02%	2.64%	7.28%	14.33%	31.13%	25.41%	27.29%	0.89%	1.00%
M	84.05%	0.02%	2.53%	6.81%	13.36%	20.59%	25.98%	28.82%	0.91%	0.99%
F	15.95%	0.01%	3.25%	9.76%	19.45%	24.03%	22.42%	19.25%	0.80%	1.03%
Secure Custody (12.99%)										
T	9,720 (100%)	—	0.40%	2.92%	10.40%	20.72%	28.43%	34.84%	1.24%	1.05%
M	92.74%	—	0.38%	2.73%	9.78%	20.15%	28.89%	35.79%	1.25%	1.03%
F	7.26%	—	0.71%	5.38%	18.27%	28.05%	22.52%	22.66%	1.13%	1.27%
Detention for Treatment										
T	11 (100%)	—	—	9.09%	27.27%	27.27%	18.18%	18.18%	—	—
M	90.91%	—	—	10.00%	30.00%	30.00%	10.00%	20.00%	—	—
F	9.09%	—	—	—	—	—	100.0%	—	—	—
Open Custody (16.7%)										
T	12,578 (100%)	0.01%	1.88%	6.47%	14.46%	23.18%	27.10%	25.11%	0.37%	1.42%
M	88.33%	0.01%	1.75%	5.95%	13.36%	22.77%	28.07%	26.35%	0.33%	1.40%
F	11.67%	—	2.86%	10.42%	22.82%	26.29%	19.75%	15.67%	0.68%	1.50%
Probation (41.6%)										
T	31,268 (100%)	0.02%	3.44%	9.04%	15.66%	21.21%	24.96%	24.55%	0.45%	0.68%
M	82.26%	0.03%	3.42%	8.67%	14.77%	20.77%	25.32%	25.92%	0.44%	0.67%
F	17.74%	—	3.53%	10.76%	19.78%	22.27%	23.27%	18.17%	0.49%	0.72%
Fine (7.9%)										
T	5,959 (100%)	0.03%	0.50%	2.23%	5.99%	13.19%	27.79%	46.69%	3.36%	0.22%
M	85.43%	0.04%	0.43%	1.92%	5.36%	12.34%	27.58%	48.60%	3.54%	0.20%
F	17.05%	—	0.92%	4.03%	9.68%	18.20%	29.03%	35.48%	2.30%	0.35%
Compensation (0.3%)										
T	245 (100%)	—	1.22%	4.08%	14.29%	22.04%	21.22%	36.33%	0.41%	0.41%
M	90.61%	—	1.35%	3.60%	12.61%	21.62%	21.17%	38.74%	0.45%	0.45%
F	9.39%	—	—	8.70%	30.34%	26.09%	21.74%	13.04%	—	—

Table 3.3 (continued)

MOST SIGNIFICANT DISPOSITION	TOTAL	AGE								
		<12	12	13	14	15	16	17	>17	UNKNOWN
Pay Purchaser										
T	38 (100%)	—	—	—	5.26%	10.53%	31.58%	52.63%	—	—
M	89.47%	—	—	—	5.88%	8.82%	32.35%	52.94%	—	—
F	10.53%	—	—	—	—	25.00%	25.00%	50.00%	—	—
Compensation (Kind)										
T	25 (100%)	—	—	8.00%	8.00%	24.00%	28.00%	32.00%	—	—
M	84.00%	—	—	9.52%	4.76%	23.81%	33.33%	28.51%	—	—
F	16.00%	—	—	—	25.00%	25.00%	—	50.00%	—	—
Community Service Order (12.5%)										
T	9,427 (100%)	0.04%	3.67%	8.82%	18.27%	24.44%	21.69%	20.74%	0.75%	1.58%
M	80.33%	0.04%	3.59%	8.53%	17.55%	23.94%	22.10%	21.80%	0.79%	1.65%
F	19.67%	0.05%	3.99%	9.98%	21.20%	26.48%	20.01%	16.40%	0.59%	1.29%
Restitution										
T	163 (100%)	—	2.45%	5.52%	12.27%	23.93%	22.09%	29.45%	3.68%	0.61%
M	90.18%	—	2.72%	4.08%	12.93%	25.17%	20.41%	29.93%	4.08%	0.68%
F	9.82%	—	—	18.75%	6.25%	12.50%	37.50%	25.00%	—	—
Prohibition/Seizure/Forfeiture										
T	68 (100%)	—	—	7.35%	7.35%	20.59%	23.53%	39.71%	1.47%	—
M	94.12%	—	—	7.81%	7.81%	21.88%	18.75%	42.19%	1.56%	—
F	5.88%	—	—	—	—	—	100.0%	—	—	—
Absolute Discharge (4.2%)										
T	3,127 (100%)	0.03%	5.18%	10.07%	15.51%	19.38%	22.74%	25.14%	0.83%	1.12%
M	70.55%	0.05%	5.53%	9.84%	14.96%	18.27%	23.30%	26.20%	0.86%	1.00%
F	29.45%	—	4.34%	10.64%	16.83%	22.04%	21.39%	22.58%	0.76%	1.41%
Other (3.3%)										
T	2,514 (100%)	—	3.58%	9.67%	16.43%	20.01%	23.11%	22.79%	2.15%	2.27%
M	77.29%	—	3.40%	9.47%	14.62%	18.53%	24.19%	25.42%	2.11%	2.26%
F	22.71%	—	4.20%	10.33%	22.59%	25.04%	19.44%	13.84%	2.28%	2.28%

seventeen-year-old age category. This finding indicates that girls come to the courts at least two years before boys; the question is, then, whether they commit crimes at an earlier age or are simply detected at an earlier age than boys. As well, a comparison of the relative proportions of males and females across decision categories indicates that the courts vary in their responses to gender categories. For example, the overall proportion of males to females is 82.3 to 17.7. For not-guilty decisions, however, males are relatively more numerous (87 per cent) and females are somewhat underrepresented (13 per cent). Conversely, for the categories of withdrawn and dismissed, female youth are relatively numerous (19.5 per cent and 22.3 per cent, respectively).

Table 3.3 provides information on all cases heard according to the most significant disposition broken down by the age and the sex of the offender.

This table is especially relevant in analysing the working of the youth courts in the context of the Young Offenders Act. One of the major principles of the act is that youth should be treated with the least invasive dispositions in the interests of their needs as citizens with rights, and with regard to their needs as persons in a state of dependency and psychological and physical development (see section 3,(1),a, e, and f, YOA [Appendix I]). Given the spirit of least intervention in the Young Offenders Act, it is interesting that expected dispositions like community service orders, compensation, and restitution are used relatively infrequently. Community service orders account for 9427 of 75,143 cases (12.5 per cent), and cases involving compensation and restitution are notably absent. Further, the majority of dispositions involve secure and open custody and probation. These three categories of disposition involve rather strict supervision and are, at first glance, in contravention of the spirit of the Young Offenders Act. In addition, section 20 (1)(a) of the YOA (Appendix I) specifies that absolute discharge is to be used if the court considers such an outcome is in the best interests of the youth. From the data in Table 3.3, it is quite clear that absolute discharges are not commonplace, and that custody and probation are used in the vast majority of cases. It is possible, however, that the legal practice of alternative measures diverts many youths from the courts before they become legal statistics. Despite this possibility, it is nonetheless noteworthy that the vast majority of dispositions involve protracted scrutiny. I argue, in the following chapters, that dispositions involving continual surveillance are the most debilitating and stigmatizing, and, as Labelling Theory suggests, the most influential in fostering further criminal behaviour for young offenders.

Table 3.3 also shows that types of dispositions vary according to age and gender. Firstly, as we will see in Table 3.4, fines, restitution, compensation, and secure custody are the most likely dispositions for older youths, while open custody, probation, community service, and absolute discharge are employed more often amongst younger offenders. Most noticeable in Table 3.3, however, are the differences across gender categories. For example, the most predominant age category for males in closed or open custody is sixteen or seventeen, while for females is fourteen or fifteen. In addition, proportionately more younger female youths receive probation and community service orders than their male counterparts. Finally, absolute discharge is most likely for younger females and older males. These trends illustrate, quite clearly, that the courts assume different views of age and gender in sentencing, and that, overall, the harshest sentences are reserved for older males and younger females.

Table 3.4 illustrates sentencing decisions by age for those youth found to be guilty.

Firstly, and most noticeable here, is the relatively large proportion of cases in which the sentence is probation (52.5 per cent). In addition, for probationary sentences, seven to twelve months is the predominant length. The predominant sentence category for open and closed custody is one to three months. It is interesting that while custody is a harsher sentence than probation, and is usually the result of a more serious offence or of a repeat offence, the accountability to the justice system for custodial decisions is shorter than for probationary outcomes. Secondly, fines, while relatively rare as dispositions, are given primarily to the oldest offenders and very rarely to twelve- to fourteen-year-olds. This is also true of closed custody, although closed custody is used somewhat more for younger offenders than are fines. Furthermore, these figures reveal that open custody and probation are used relatively more often for younger offenders than are fines or closed custody.

Table 3.5 presents cases heard by youth courts in Canada relating decision to most significant charge, again for males and females.

Most significantly for violent offences, the overwhelming decision outcome is guilty; the not-guilty decisions are remarkably infrequent. As well, cases dismissed and charges withdrawn combine to comprise almost 25 per cent of the outcomes. The percentages in each category of violent offences for males and females are surprisingly similar. For specific violent offences, however, the trends change somewhat. For example, guilty decisions for murder are less frequent than guilty decisions overall, and a sizeable number of these cases are transferred to adult court. Once again, however, approximately 19 per cent of murder cases end in charges being withdrawn, a somewhat surprising phenomenon. Sexual assault is somewhat anomalous to the other violent offences; the charges dismissed, charges withdrawn, and not-guilty findings for sexual assault are relatively high, especially in comparison to assault. Obviously the courts are less likely to treat cases of sexual assault as being as valid and legitimate as those of assault and robbery. The percentages of assault are almost identical to those for overall violent offences. The data for robbery, however, do present another anomalous finding. The percentage of guilty decisions for females is markedly smaller than for males, and the percentage for withdrawn charges is much larger for females than males. The courts obviously treat male robbery as much more serious and are inclined to use the full weight of the law against males relative to females.

For property offences we see, once again, that males and females are treated differently. Where the percentage differences between males and females were almost negligible for total number of violent offences, the differences are quite apparent for overall property offences. For example, guilty decisions are much

Table 3.4 Cases Heard with Guilty Findings by Youth Court in Canada by Length of Sentence and Dollar Amount of Most Significant Disposition and Age of the Accused, 1991–92

MOST SIGNIFICANT DISPOSITION	TOTAL	AGE								
		<12	12	13	14	15	16	17	>17	UNKNOWN
SECURE CUSTODY (16.3%)										
Total	9,720 (100%)	—	0.40%	2.92%	10.40%	20.72%	28.43%	34.84%	1.24%	1.05%
<Months	26.29%	—	0.63%	2.90%	10.49%	20.23%	28.06%	33.86%	2.58%	1.25%
1–3 Months	44.39%	—	0.32%	2.71%	11.43%	20.86%	27.67%	34.95%	1.14%	0.93%
4–6 Months	16.89%	—	0.43%	3.71%	10.60%	20.52%	28.38%	35.01%	0.18%	1.16%
7–12 Months	9.14%	—	0.11%	3.04%	6.53%	20.72%	32.55%	35.59%	0.23%	1.24%
13–24 Months	2.95%	—	—	1.74%	5.23%	24.74%	31.01%	36.93%	0.35%	—
>24 Months	0.34%	—	3.03%	—	9.09%	15.15%	24.24%	48.48%	—	—
OPEN CUSTODY (21.2%)										
Total	12,578 (100%)	0.01%	1.88%	6.47%	14.46%	23.18%	27.10%	25.11%	0.37%	1.42%
<1 Month	19.82%	—	2.21%	7.90%	15.08%	23.23%	23.99%	25.23%	0.88%	1.48%
1–3 Months	48.21%	—	1.52%	5.94%	14.56%	23.48%	28.08%	24.70%	0.25%	1.47%
4–6 Months	22.67%	—	2.21%	6.87%	14.27%	23.28%	26.82%	25.18%	0.25%	1.16%
7–12 Months	8.35%	0.10%	2.10%	5.05%	13.52%	21.33%	29.43%	26.29%	0.29%	1.90%
13–24 Months	0.86%	—	3.70%	7.41%	9.26%	20.37%	29.63%	29.63%	—	—
>24 Months	0.09%	—	—	—	9.09%	27.27%	18.18%	45.45%	—	—

Table 3.4 (continued)

MOST SIGNIFICANT DISPOSITION	TOTAL	AGE								
		<12	12	13	14	15	16	17	>17	UNKNOWN
PROBATION (52.5%)										
Total	31,268 (100%)	0.02%	3.44%	9.04%	15.66%	21.21%	24.96%	24.55%	0.45%	0.68%
<1 Month	0.19%	—	1.67%	3.33%	8.33%	21.67%	30.00%	26.67%	—	8.33%
1–3 Months	5.20%	—	3.69%	9.90%	16.23%	22.56%	23.48%	22.86%	0.86%	0.43%
4–6 Months	28.82%	0.03%	3.22%	9.01%	15.71%	21.56%	23.70%	25.77%	0.54%	0.44%
7–12 Months	50.32%	0.03%	3.34%	8.85%	15.52%	21.19%	25.72%	24.28%	0.40%	0.67%
13–24 Months	15.38%	—	4.10%	9.46%	15.88%	20.15%	25.32%	23.66%	0.31%	1.12%
>24 Months	0.08%	—	3.85%	11.54%	19.23%	23.08%	11.54%	30.77%	—	—
FINE (10.0%)										
Total	5,959 (100%)	0.03%	0.50%	2.23%	5.99%	13.19%	27.79%	46.69%	3.36%	0.22%
< $50	12.77%	—	0.66%	5.26%	8.28%	18.53%	27.20%	35.74%	4.20%	0.13%
$50–100	47.14%	0.07%	0.75%	2.56%	7.30%	14.49%	27.84%	42.61%	4.24%	0.14%
$101–500	38.78%	—	0.17%	0.91%	3.85%	10.21%	28.30%	54.13%	2.08%	0.35%
> $500	2.08%	—	—	—	—	2.56%	16.67%	79.49%	1.28%	—

Table 3.5 Cases Heard by Youth Courts in Canada by Most Significant Decision and Most Significant Charge, 1991–92

MOST SIGNIFICANT CHARGE		TOTAL	MOST SIGNIFICANT DECISION							
			TRANSFER TO ADULT COURT	GUILTY	NOT GUILTY	PROCEEDINGS STAYED	DISMISSED	WITHDRAWN	TRANSFER OF JURISDICTION	OTHER
TOTAL	T	116,397 (100%)	0.06%	64.56%	1.30%	7.13%	4.02%	22.82%	0.07%	0.04%
	M	82.31%	0.07%	65.92%	1.38%	7.03%	3.93%	21.56%	0.08%	0.04%
	F	17.69%	0.01%	58.21%	0.96%	7.58%	4.43%	28.71%	0.05%	0.06%
VIOLENT OFFENCES	T	18,800 (100%)	0.18%	64.19%	2.58%	7.82%	5.48%	19.69%	0.03%	0.03%
	M	81.72%	0.21%	64.35%	2.73%	7.64%	5.64%	19.35%	0.03%	0.03%
	F	18.28%	—	63.45%	1.89%	8.64%	4.77%	21.22%	—	0.03%
Murder/Manslaughter	T	48 (100%)	16.67%	52.08%	2.08%	6.25%	4.17%	18.75%	—	—
	M	87.50%	19.05%	50.00%	2.38%	7.14%	2.38%	19.05%	—	—
	F	12.50%	—	66.67%	—	—	16.67%	16.67%	—	—
Sexual Assault	T	1,521 (100%)	0.59%	57.53%	4.87%	11.57%	8.55%	16.77%	0.07%	0.07%
	M	97.90%	0.60%	57.56%	4.90%	11.62%	8.60%	16.59%	0.07%	0.07%
	F	2.10%	—	56.25%	3.13%	9.38%	6.25%	25.00%	—	—
Assault	T	12,190 (100%)	0.07%	66.13%	2.33%	7.11%	5.12%	19.20%	0.02%	0.03%
	M	75.73%	0.09%	66.41%	2.47%	6.71%	5.31%	18.97%	0.02%	0.03%
	F	24.27%	—	65.26%	1.89%	8.38%	4.53%	19.91%	—	0.03%

Table 3.5 (continued)

MOST SIGNIFICANT CHARGE		TOTAL	TRANSFER TO ADULT COURT	MOST SIGNIFICANT DECISION						
				GUILTY	NOT GUILTY	PROCEEDINGS STAYED	DISMISSED	WITHDRAWN	TRANSFER OF JURISDICTION	OTHER
Robbery	T	2,070 (100%)	0.29%	62.95%	2.80%	7.29%	4.54%	22.08%	0.05%	—
	M	86.67%	0.33%	65.05%	2.90%	7.02%	4.35%	20.29%	0.06%	—
	F	13.33%	—	49.28%	2.17%	9.06%	5.80%	33.70%	—	—
PROPERTY OFFENCES	T	66,632 (100%)	0.05%	64.73%	1.04%	6.36%	4.33%	23.34%	0.10%	0.05%
	M	83.74%	0.05%	67.02%	1.06%	6.32%	4.06%	21.33%	0.11%	0.05%
	F	16.26%	0.03%	52.95%	0.91%	6.58%	5.71%	33.67%	0.09%	0.06%
Break and Enter	T	16,653 (100%)	0.14%	76.03%	1.12%	6.55%	3.01%	12.95%	0.14%	0.07%
	M	93.77%	0.13%	76.72%	1.10%	6.29%	2.94%	12.60%	0.14%	0.06%
	F	6.23%	0.19%	65.57%	1.45%	10.41%	4.05%	18.13%	0.10%	0.10%
Motor Vehicle Theft	T	1,557 (100%)	—	73.22%	0.32%	5.01%	3.73%	17.41%	0.26%	0.06%
	M	83.69%	—	74.60%	0.38%	4.83%	3.53%	16.35%	0.23%	0.08%
	F	16.31%	—	66.14%	—	5.91%	4.72%	22.83%	0.39%	—
Theft >$1,000	T	3,860 (100%)	0.05%	70.75%	1.63%	8.47%	3.16%	15.70%	0.12%	0.03%
	M	91.14%	0.06%	71.92%	1.73%	8.27%	3.01%	14.78%	0.20%	0.03%
	F	8.86%	—	58.77%	0.58%	10.53%	4.68%	25.15%	0.29%	—
Theft <$1,000	T	23,840 (100%)	0.01%	57.85%	0.84%	5.68%	5.32%	30.18%	0.08%	0.04%
	M	73.36%	0.01%	61.31%	0.84%	5.67%	4.95%	27.11%	0.07%	0.04%
	F	26.64%	—	48.34%	0.83%	5.72%	6.36%	38.64%	0.08%	0.03%

Table 3.5 (continued)

MOST SIGNIFICANT CHARGE	TOTAL	TRANSFER TO ADULT COURT	GUILTY	NOT GUILTY	PROCEEDINGS STAYED	DISMISSED	WITHDRAWN	TRANSFER OF JURISDICTION	OTHER
Possession of Stolen Property									
T	9,506 (100%)	0.02%	63.68%	0.95%	6.52%	4.21%	24.52%	0.08%	0.02%
M	88.67%	0.02%	64.72%	0.93%	6.67%	3.97%	23.59%	0.08%	0.02%
F	11.33%	—	55.52%	1.11%	5.39%	6.04%	31.85%	0.09%	—
OTHER CRIMINAL CODE									
T	19,053 (100%)	0.03%	62.07%	1.14%	6.57%	2.69%	27.43%	0.02%	0.04%
M	79.37%	0.04%	62.37%	1.32%	6.34%	2.72%	27.17%	0.03%	0.02%
F	20.63%	—	60.95%	0.46%	7.48%	2.57%	28.44%	—	0.10%
Impaired Operation									
T	1,270 (100%)	—	83.94%	2.91%	3.07%	2.76%	7.32%	—	—
M	88.50%	—	84.43%	3.02%	2.94%	2.49%	7.12%	—	—
F	11.50%	—	80.14%	2.05%	4.11%	4.79%	8.90%	—	—
Unlawfully at Large/Failure to Appear									
T	10,793 (100%)	0.02%	56.61%	0.37%	7.49%	1.87%	33.62%	0.02%	—
M	77.46%	0.02%	56.53%	0.43%	7.25%	1.97%	33.78%	0.02%	—
F	22.54%	—	56.88%	0.16%	8.30%	1.52%	33.13%	—	—
Soliciting									
T	373 (100%)	—	78.55%	—	5.63%	1.61%	13.94%	—	0.27%
M	8.31%	—	54.84%	—	6.45%	—	38.71%	—	—
F	91.69%	—	80.70%	—	5.56%	1.75%	11.70%	—	0.29%

Table 3.5 (continued)

MOST SIGNIFICANT CHARGE	TOTAL	TRANSFER TO ADULT COURT	MOST SIGNIFICANT DECISION						
			GUILTY	NOT GUILTY	PROCEEDINGS STAYED	DISMISSED	WITH-DRAWN	TRANSFER OF JURISDICTION	OTHER
NARCOTIC CONTROL ACT									
T	2,027 (100%)	0.05%	69.12%	1.68%	6.36%	4.44%	18.30%	0.05%	—
M	84.76%	0.06%	70.78%	1.57%	5.76%	4.54%	17.23%	0.06%	—
F	15.24%	—	59.87%	2.27%	9.71%	3.88%	24.27%	—	—
Trafficking in Narcotics									
T	637 (100%)	—	71.27%	3.14%	5.65%	5.35%	14.44%	0.16%	—
M	86.50%	—	73.14%	2.90%	4.90%	5.63%	13.25%	0.18%	—
F	13.50%	—	59.30%	4.65%	10.47%	3.49%	22.09%	—	—
Possession of Narcotics									
T	1,363 (100%)	0.07%	67.79%	0.95%	6.82%	4.04%	20.32%	—	—
M	84.59%	0.09%	69.56%	0.95%	6.24%	3.99%	19.17%	—	—
F	15.41%	—	58.10%	0.95%	10.00%	4.29%	26.67%	—	—
YOUNG OFFENDERS ACT									
T	9,418 (100%)	0.01%	67.62%	0.92%	12.48%	1.53%	17.36%	0.07%	0.01%
M	78.52%	0.01%	66.52%	1.07%	12.89%	1.73%	17.69%	0.09%	—
F	21.48%	—	71.63%	0.40%	10.97%	0.79%	16.16%	—	0.05%
Failure to Comply with a Disposition									
T	9,401 (100%)	0.01%	67.63%	0.91%	12.48%	1.53%	17.35%	0.07%	0.01%
M	78.51%	0.01%	66.54%	1.06%	12.88%	1.73%	17.68%	0.09%	—
F	21.49%	—	71.63%	0.40%	10.99%	0.79%	16.14%	—	0.05%

less common for women, and case-withdrawn outcomes are more common. As with robbery, the courts appear to view the property offences of women as less threatening than those of men. An alternative explanation may be that a greater proportion of the male property offenders are repeat offenders relative to women, although here I speculate. The differences noted between males and females are consistent for the other categories of property offences. It is worth noting, too, that among all the categories of property offences, some cases do go to adult court (especially break and enter) although the percentages are relatively small. Further, a sizeable proportion of charges for all types of property offences are withdrawn.

The categories of other offences present some further inconsistencies in how the law views male and female offences. While the percentage differences between males and females are similar for impaired driving and for being unlawfully at large, the differences for soliciting are astonishing. Although there are few cases of male solicitation, only 54.84 per cent of these cases end in guilty decisions compared to 80.7 per cent for females. Further, charges withdrawn are markedly higher for males than females. Where the courts tend to treat property crimes for females less seriously than for males, it appears that the opposite is true of soliciting. This may reflect traditional legal presumptions that prostitution is most harmful to a society when practised by females. Contrary to that trend are Narcotics Control Act violations in which women receive relatively fewer guilty decisions and greater proportions of withdrawn charges. These differences are consistent for trafficking and possession.

Lastly in Table 3.5, the violations which reflect non-compliance with court orders and contraventions of the Young Offenders Act orders are treated rather harshly. For example, for the offence of failure to comply with a disposition, the proportions of guilty decisions are relatively large, and more interestingly, larger for females than males. However, for the category of unlawfully at large/failure to appear, the courts appear to be more lenient, with smaller proportions of guilty decisions and greater proportions of withdrawn charges. Further comment on these acts of defiance follows in the discussions for Table 3.6.

The last comment I wish to make about the results in Table 3.5 is in relation to those cases transferred to adult court. Recently, there has been a concerted backlash against the Young Offenders Act for being too lenient, especially in relation to violent offenders. The act, say its detractors, is mandated to deal too leniently with dangerous offenders. The findings in this table indicate that the act does have and does use provisions which account for the seriousness of the offence through transfer to adult jurisdiction. We see from this table that some cases—especially murder, sexual assault, robbery, and break and enter—are handled in adult courts where the seriousness of the crime can be assessed and responded to with more appropriate severity than permitted under the Young Offenders Act. The panic over young offenders literally 'getting away with murder' is not substantiated by the findings in this table.

Table 3.6 presents data on the types of penalties given by youth courts for different types of offences for males and females.

This table gives some indication of how the spirit of the Young Offenders Act has been applied. For example, for less serious crimes, the expectation is that custodial dispositions should be minimal, and that probation, compensation, and community service orders would be relatively numerous. For total offences, the use of probation is relatively high, while the use of community service is appreciably lower. Further, the use of open and closed custody represents almost 30 per cent of the overall dispositions. It is interesting that male and female dispositions are dissimilar, with males receiving greater proportions of custodial dispositions and females receiving more probation, community service, and absolute discharge dispositions.

The aforementioned trends, however, change according to the type of offence. For example, while the trends for all violent offences are similar to the trends for total offences, the trends for murder are markedly different. For murder/ manslaughter, 75 per cent of the female offenders and 47 per cent of male offenders receive closed custody. While the overall number of offences is small, the disparities in sentencing give us some sense that murder is considered by the courts to be especially heinous for female offenders. The other types of violent offences, however, are not consistent with this finding. For offences like assault and robbery, female offenders receive less custodial dispositions and more probation orders than males. The offence of sexual assault is interesting in that while the number of female offenders is relatively small (2.07 per cent), female offenders are treated especially leniently, with the vast majority receiving proba- tion (77.78 per cent). Males receive higher rates of secure and open custody and lower rates of probation. The difference may reflect the perceived or real differ- ences in violence and harm in sexual assaults committed by males and females.

When we observe the total dispositions for sexual assault compared to other violent offences, it is quite clear that the courts, in a very traditional manner, treat cases of sexual assault as a less serious form of violence. Fifty-eight per cent of the convicted sexual assailants received probation, compared to 48.61 per cent for non-sexual assailants and 34.16 per cent for those convicted of robbery. Quite clearly, in the eyes of youth court, among violent offences the most serious are murder and robbery, and the least serious are sexual assault offences.

The trends in dispositions by gender for all property offences are remarkably similar to those for violent offences. Once again, males receive higher rates of open and closed custody and lower rates of probation and community service. The specific property offences, break and enter and theft over $1000 receive the highest rates of custody. The differences between males and females are consis- tent with those found for overall property offences.

The categories of other criminal code offences and Narcotics Control Act offences present some interesting anomalies in sentencing. For example, the rates of custodial sentences for soliciting are higher for females than males as are rates for fines. These sentences may reflect the traditional view of prostitution held by the courts that (a) the problems of prostitution that disturb the society are created primarily by females, and (b) that young, female prostitutes need

Table 3.6 Cases Heard by Youth Courts in Canada by Most Significant Disposition and Offence, by Sex of the Accused, 1991-92

OFFENCE	TOTAL	MOST SIGNIFICANT DISPOSITION									
		SECURE CUSTODY	OPEN CUSTODY	PROBATION	FINE	COMPEN-SATION	PAY PURCHASER	COMPEN-SATION	COMMUNITY SERVICE	ABSOLUTE DISCHARGE	OTHER
TOTAL											
T	75,143 (100%)	12.94%	16.74%	41.61%	7.93%	0.33%	0.05%	0.03%	12.55%	4.16%	3.67%
M	84.05%	14.27%	17.59%	40.73%	8.06%	0.35%	0.05%	0.03%	11.99%	3.49%	3.43%
F	15.95%	5.89%	12.25%	46.28%	7.24%	0.19%	0.03%	0.03%	15.47%	7.68%	4.96%
VIOLENT OFFENCES											
T	11,828 (100%)	13.33%	15.84%	47.51%	3.80%	0.08%	—	0.01%	12.45%	4.16%	2.82%
M	81.77%	15.00%	17.03%	45.62%	4.02%	0.09%	—	0.01%	11.77%	3.69%	2.77%
F	18.23%	5.84%	10.84%	56.03%	2.78%	0.05%	—	—	15.49%	6.26%	3.06%
Murder/Manslaughter											
T	25 (100%)	52.00%	24.00%	16.00%	—	—	—	—	8.00%	—	—
M	84.00%	47.62%	28.57%	14.29%	—	—	—	—	9.52%	—	—
F	16.00%	75.00%	—	25.00%	—	—	—	—	—	—	—
Sexual Assault											
T	869 (100%)	14.38%	19.22%	58.00%	0.23%	—	—	—	5.06%	1.61%	1.50%
M	97.93%	14.57%	19.27%	57.58%	0.24%	—	—	—	5.17%	1.65%	1.53%
F	2.07%	5.56%	16.67%	77.78%	—	—	—	—	—	—	—
Assault											
T	7,877 (100%)	10.37%	14.61%	48.61%	4.63%	0.06%	—	0.01%	13.91%	4.82%	2.96%
M	75.78%	12.08%	16.15%	46.12%	5.13%	0.07%	—	0.02%	13.34%	4.19%	2.92%
F	24.22%	5.03%	9.80%	56.39%	3.09%	0.05%	—	—	15.72%	6.81%	3.09%
Robbery											
T	1,297 (100%)	31.77%	23.59%	34.16%	1.00%	0.15%	—	—	8.40%	0.62%	0.31%
M	89.59%	33.65%	24.35%	32.27%	1.03%	0.17%	—	—	7.49%	0.69%	0.34%
F	10.41%	15.56%	17.04%	50.37%	0.74%	—	—	—	16.30%	—	—

Table 3.6 (continued)

OFFENCE	TOTAL	MOST SIGNIFICANT DISPOSITION									
		SECURE CUSTODY	OPEN CUSTODY	PROBATION	FINE	COMPEN-SATION	PAY PURCHASER	COMPEN-SATION	COMMUNITY SERVICE	ABSOLUTE DISCHARGE	OTHER
PROPERTY OFFENCES											
T	42,867 (100%)	10.55%	15.34%	46.52%	5.80%	0.50%	0.06%	0.05%	13.49%	4.59%	3.09%
M	86.66%	11.76%	16.36%	45.93%	5.68%	0.52%	0.06%	0.05%	12.88%	3.78%	2.97%
F	13.34%	2.69%	8.66%	50.38%	6.63%	0.37%	0.07%	0.07%	17.44%	9.81%	3.88%
Break and Enter											
T	12,593 (100%)	17.71%	20.44%	47.72%	1.46%	0.25%	0.03%	0.01%	9.44%	1.02%	1.91%
M	94.67%	18.43%	20.81%	46.83%	1.48%	0.25%	0.03%	0.01%	9.32%	0.94%	1.90%
F	5.33%	4.92%	13.86%	63.64%	1.04%	0.15%	—	—	11.62%	2.53%	2.24%
Motor Vehicle Theft											
T	1,109 (100%)	4.51%	12.44%	54.37%	4.42%	0.18%	—	—	15.24%	5.32%	3.52%
M	85.03%	5.30%	13.47%	53.34%	4.67%	0.11%	—	—	14.10%	5.41%	3.61%
F	14.97%	—	6.63%	60.24%	3.01%	0.60%	—	—	21.69%	4.82%	3.01%
Theft > $1,000											
T	2,690 (100%)	17.88%	19.93%	45.20%	3.49%	0.26%	0.07%	—	9.67%	2.12%	1.38%
M	92.68%	18.81%	20.18%	44.28%	3.65%	0.24%	0.08%	—	9.43%	1.93%	1.40%
F	7.32%	6.09%	16.75%	56.85%	1.52%	0.51%	—	—	12.69%	4.57%	1.02%
Theft < $1,000											
T	13,361 (100%)	4.07%	10.67%	45.90%	10.40%	0.38%	0.07%	0.06%	16.85%	8.19%	3.32%
M	77.57%	4.79%	12.04%	45.72%	10.70%	0.42%	0.08%	0.06%	16.14%	6.79%	3.28%
F	22.43%	1.60%	5.92%	46.55%	9.75%	0.26%	0.07%	0.07%	19.30%	13.05%	3.43%
Possession of Stolen Property											
T	6,085 (100%)	11.98%	17.24%	43.11%	5.88%	0.28%	0.05%	0.02%	13.94%	3.76%	3.75%
M	90.07%	12.97%	17.95%	42.13%	6.08%	0.27%	0.05%	0.02%	13.88%	3.27%	3.56%
F	9.93%	4.64%	10.76%	51.99%	4.14%	0.33%	—	—	14.40%	8.28%	5.46%

Table 3.6 (continued)

OFFENCE	TOTAL	SECURE CUSTODY	OPEN CUSTODY	PROBATION	FINE	COMPEN-SATION	PAY PURCHASER	COMPEN-SATION	COMMUNITY SERVICE	ABSOLUTE DISCHARGE	OTHER
										MOST SIGNIFICANT DISPOSITION	
OTHER CRIMINAL CODE											
T	12,102 (100%)	18.49%	20.51%	28.95%	13.40%	0.06%	0.06%	0.01%	9.21%	3.12%	6.20%
M	80.03%	20.34%	21.52%	26.90%	14.31%	0.07%	0.07%	0.01%	8.88%	2.43%	5.47%
F	19.97%	11.09%	16.47%	37.19%	9.76%	—	—	—	10.51%	5.88	9.10%
Impaired Operation											
T	1,065 (100%)	2.44%	4.13%	28.73%	58.59%	—	—	—	5.26%	—	0.58%
M	88.92%	2.64%	4.22%	27.35%	59.66%	—	—	—	5.28%	—	0.84%
F	11.08%	0.85%	3.39%	39.83%	50.00%	—	—	—	5.08%	—	0.85%
Unlawfully at Large/Failure to Appear											
T	6,163 (100%)	19.67%	27.79%	22.12%	9.07%	—	0.02%	0.02%	9.41%	3.00%	8.92%
M	77.66%	21.37%	29.23%	20.16%	9.34%	—	0.02%	0.02%	9.15%	2.34%	8.00%
F	22.34%	12.49%	22.80%	28.83%	8.13%	—	—	—	10.31%	5.30%	12.13%
Soliciting											
T	294 (100%)	3.05%	5.78%	63.27%	9.18%	—	—	—	3.40%	10.88%	4.42%
M	5.78%	—	5.88%	64.71%	5.88%	—	—	—	—	11.76%	11.76%
F	94.22%	3.25%	5.78%	63.18%	9.39%	—	—	—	3.61%	10.83%	3.97%
NARCOTIC CONTROL ACT											
T	1,347 (100%)	14.03%	14.18%	34.74%	18.86%	0.15%	—	—	8.46%	7.72%	1.86%
M	86.64%	14.82%	14.48%	33.76%	19.88%	0.17%	—	—	7.63%	7.46%	1.80%
F	13.36%	8.89%	12.22%	41.11%	12.22%	—	—	—	13.89%	9.44%	2.22%
Trafficking in Narcotics											
T	454 (100%)	23.35%	17.40%	41.19%	7.05%	—	—	—	8.81%	1.10%	1.10%
M	88.55%	24.88%	17.91%	40.80%	7.21%	—	—	—	7.21%	0.75%	1.24%
F	11.45%	11.54%	13.46%	44.23%	5.77%	—	—	—	21.15%	3.85%	—

Table 3.6 (continued)

OFFENCE	TOTAL	MOST SIGNIFICANT DISPOSITION									
		SECURE CUSTODY	OPEN CUSTODY	PROBATION	FINE	COMPEN-SATION	PAY PURCHASER	COMPEN-SATION	COMMUNITY SERVICE	ABSOLUTE DISCHARGE	OTHER
Possession of Narcotics											
T	869 (100%)	8.52%	11.62%	32.11%	25.43%	0.23%	—	—	8.40%	11.39%	2.30%
M	86.65%	9.16%	12.08%	30.41%	26.83%	0.27%	—	—	7.97%	11.16%	2.12%
F	13.35%	4.31%	8.62%	43.10%	16.38%	—	—	—	11.21%	12.93%	3.45%
YOUNG OFFENDERS ACT											
T	6,654 (100%)	17.69%	21.70%	24.06%	14.74%	0.17%	0.06%	0.02%	13.84%	2.52%	4.66%
M	77.82%	19.99%	21.57%	22.56%	15.93%	0.19%	0.08%	0.02%	13.17%	2.05%	4.44%
F	22.18%	9.62%	22.15%	31.76%	10.57%	0.07%	—	—	16.19%	4.20%	5.42%
Failure to Comply with a Disposition											
T	6,644 (100%)	17.67%	21.73%	24.58%	14.75%	0.17%	0.06%	0.02%	13.83%	2.53%	4.67%
M	77.81%	19.96%	21.61%	22.55%	15.94%	0.19%	0.08%	0.02%	13.15%	2.05%	4.45%
F	22.19%	9.63%	22.18%	31.68%	10.58%	0.07%	—	—	16.21%	4.21%	5.43%

legal intervention for their own safety. For narcotics offences, males are treated more severely than females. For the category of trafficking, for example, 21.15 per cent of females compared to 7.21 per cent of males receive community service, while males receive twice the rate of closed custody. The same differences appear for possession, with the exception 'that fines are much more predominant for possession than for trafficking and that males receive proportionately more fines and fewer probation orders than females. Here, unlike the case of prostitution, the courts presume that there is more danger to society from male than female offenders and that dispositions should reflect that danger.

Offences that are in defiance of court procedure and decisions, such as failure to appear and failure to comply with a disposition, are relatively common, and in Table 3.6 the ratio of males to females is smaller, with few exceptions, than for all other offences. Approximately 12 per cent of all female offenders fall into the two categories of defiance compared to only 8 per cent of all male offenders. This shows quite clearly, I argue, that the legal system is somewhat more intimidating for male offenders, and that there may be some justification for this belief. For example, if we observe differences in disposition for unlawfully at large/failure to appear and for failure to comply with a disposition, we see that males are punished more severely—with higher rates of custody and lower rates of probation.

Overall, these tables indicate that the decisions that are made in youth court vary according to the type of offence, the gender of the offender, and the offender's age. Further, the data also reveal that the principles and goals of diversion that underscore the Young Offenders Act are not consistently met, and that punitiveness is quite common for certain offences and offenders. Disparities in the administration of youth courts do exist and these disparities are not always legally predictable.

I have included this discussion of historical and contemporary trends in juvenile crime rates, not as a comprehensive discussion of the aftermath of the Young Offenders Act, but as an analysis of official offence rates to present a backdrop to the analysis of youth court data, to illustrate that youth crime rates are as much a function of the nature of justice (hence vulnerable to law reform) and the discretionary nature of policing and jurisprudence as they are of actual crime committed. The following chapters attempt to analyse and understand the nature of discretionary justice as applied to young offenders. The data were gathered in 1985, at the height of the development of youth court administration resulting from the Young Offenders Act.

Chapter Four attempts to explain disparities in justice from a critical/ conflict perspective. The final section of the chapter presents two issues which are fundamental to the critical position of this book. The first of these issues is that delinquent behaviour is almost universal and mostly fleeting, and that most youths have the potential 'to be caught'. The second issue is that the Young Offenders Act has, in fact, been implemented to redress inequities in youth justice that were evident with the Juvenile Delinquency Act.

chapter four

Explanations for Disparities

in Youth Justice

If, as is the contention of this book, justice is preferentially applied to young offenders, what, then, are the criteria upon which judgements are made? In this work, I attempt to parcel out the vagaries of a legal system that treats individuals differently on the bases of gender, ethnicity, and social class (Chambliss 1969; Turk 1969). Preferential treatment can be analysed at different stages of the judicial process from the initial arrest stage to the final stage of disposition. This chapter presents a theoretical discussion on youth justice as well as an overview of previous research in the area that tries to explain discriminatory justice at the different stages of the justice process. The explanations presented are especially pertinent in the context of ethnicity, class, and family power in Canada.

Conflict and Youth Crime

Studies of the causal nature of juvenile delinquency and chronic criminal behaviour generally assume that definitions and prohibitions of crime and deviance are not absolute, but that they are relative to social power manifested through socio-economic characteristics such as race, class, and gender (Havemann 1992; Reid-MacNevin 1991; West 1991). The micro-social or psychological dimension of this current of thought is subsumed under various labels such as ethnomethodology and labelling theory; the macro-social or structural component is primarily Marxist-oriented. The relativist view of rule-breaking behaviour situates the cause of such behaviour with society. The label of criminal or deviant is conferred upon an individual, not on the basis of the quality of an act, but on the basis of a social evaluation. Society's reaction to the act, then, is partly based on considerations such as the violator's age, ethnicity, and social class; in essence, we scrutinize and punish social disadvantage rather than deviant behaviour (Piliavin and Briar 1964; Cicourel 1968). Socio-economic power becomes the basis upon which society scrutinizes deviant activity: 'those people are arrested, tried and sentenced who can offer the fewest rewards for nonenforcement of the laws and who can be processed without creating any undue strain for the organizations which comprise the legal system' (Chambliss 1969). Turk (1969) echoes similar sentiments; in his statements on crime control he cites sophistication, social and economic power, and cultural congruity as determinants of enforcement of legal norms.

The history of juvenile justice as presented in Chapter One illustrates the class-based nature of legal reforms. The work of Platt (1969) and others is supported by Marxist criminologists who posit that laws are created in the interest of powerful interest groups. Quinney's Marxist political economy approach (1977), for example, suggests that the legal system originates with those who control society's economic power. Earlier theorists, such as Chambliss and Seidman (1971), Turk (1969), and Dahrendorf (1959) take a more pluralistic view of power, arguing that power struggles in the context of political bureaucracy are central to law formation. While these historical perspectives focus on law formation, the primary concern of my research is the selective application of juvenile statutes. Socio-historical accounts of law formulation are not however irrelevant. On the contrary, such research illustrates that many laws are created with the purpose of facilitating prejudicial and discriminatory application.

Discriminatory Policing

Early American criminological research documented discretion and bias at both the police and the court levels. Goldman (1963) illustrated attitudinal biases among the police towards Black juveniles, biases which consider such juveniles as less tractable and in need of more authoritarian supervision. Piliavin and Briar (1964) and Cicourel (1968) corroborated these findings by showing how police react not only to colour, but also to demeanour and deportment, that in effect, police officers prejudge juveniles on the basis of race and class. Later studies (Hirschi 1969; Williams and Gold 1972) supported previous findings, again indicating that Black and lower-class juveniles are over-represented, at least at the arrest level. Hepburn (1978) documented the impact of extra-legal variables on police decisions to arrest and court decisions to issue warrants. His findings showed that variables such as race (white/non-White) age, sex, and type of offence are correlated with decisions to arrest and warrants refused. Hepburn, however, did not control for previous record; certainly such a consideration may affect the impact of extra-legal variables.

Studies of Native juveniles in Canadian urban centres reveal that Native youth are publicly visible and are geographically located in areas of high police control. Hylton (1981) has looked at police and public attitudes towards Natives in Regina and has determined a correlation between fear of crime and negative attitudes towards Natives amongst the general public. More importantly Hylton has also found that the police hold even more stereotypical attitudes than does the public, and that these attitudes are heightened by increased contact with Natives in a policing capacity.

Hagan, Gillis, and Chan (1980) have studied the effects of socio-economic status on official delinquency using path analysis to test causal models of official rates of delinquency combining justice variables with social and demographic factors. The authors have determined the relative importance of police conceptions of crime-prone areas and citizen complaints as strong predictors of official delinquency rates. As well, they propose that socio-economic status and housing density of an area have direct effects on police conceptions, and that socio-economic status also has an indirect effect through housing density. As the authors suggest, 'actual class differences in the experience of juvenile crime are amplified by underclass housing conditions and complaint practices, and, in turn, even more so by police perceptions' (1980: 100). These findings have been checked by the authors against verbal assessments by the police regarding residential areas and delinquency. Finally, Doob and Chan (1983) have studied the nature of police decisions to arrest using data gathered from police records, field observations, and an experimental field study. Their results argue quite conclusively that the police assess both legal and situational factors in determining whether to charge a juvenile. Furthermore, the authors conclude that the justice system is such that the attitude of the juvenile is a central criterion when the police decide to lay charges.

Two points need to be emphasized here regarding police decisions to charge. First, as Doob and Chan (1983) argue, if the system is designed to demand that the police use discretion when arresting youth, then, necessarily, the attitude and deportment of the accused will be of primary importance in the decision to charge. Secondly, attitude is based partly on the degree of deference and contrition that the accused shows and on his or her ability to use social skills in avoiding arrest. I would argue, as have others (Piliavin and Briar 1964; Cicourel 1968), that when the police assess attitude, they are partly assessing ethno-cultural difference, class, and knowledge.

Support for the foregoing claims, however, is not unequivocal. Black and Reiss (1970) have documented the relationship between Black/White delinquency and seriousness of crime only to find little support for the claim that the police behave prejudicially towards Black adolescents. Lundman, Sykes, and Clark (1978) have replicated the Black and Reiss design and have reached similar conclusions. Landau (1981), in a study of Tel Aviv youth, has similarly determined that ethnicity, sex, age, and residence have very little impact on police decision to arrest. Cohen and Kluegel (1979) use a log-linear analysis on a model predicting intake screening decisions in juvenile courts in Memphis and Denver. The findings of these authors reflect no race or class bias but, again, show a strong influence of legal variables such as record and seriousness of offence.

Much of the previous research has used elaboration analyses based on cross-tabulations in assessing models of juvenile justice. Such analyses are limited to the incorporation of two or three variables in a single analysis. In an attempt to correct some of the methodological and analytical flaws that are characteristic of such research, Landau (1981) and Dannefer and Shutt (1982) have tested their models of police and judicial discretion using log-linear analytic techniques. Log-linear analysis, as we will see in Chapters Five and Six, allows for the incorporation of several categorical variables in a cross-tabular, causal model format (logit analysis).

Landau (1981) has pursued the notion of police discretion, using a sample of juvenile offenders from the Greater London area. While reinforcing the impact of legal variables, he has illustrated the additional influence that extra-legal variables such as area, age, and ethnic group have on police decisions to lay certain types of charges. Dannefer and Shutt (1982) have compared police and judicial discretion and have found a strong correlation between race and police discretion and a somewhat weaker relationship between race and judicial outcome. This weaker relationship, however, does illustrate preferential treatment of White over Black and Hispanic adolescents; Hispanic youth receive the harshest treatment of the three categories of youth. As in previous research, the authors have found strong correlations between legal variables, such as prior record and seriousness of offence, on dispositions at both levels.

An important addendum to a discussion of discriminatory policing involves the aspect of the universality of rule-breaking behaviour amongst youth. The statement that delinquency is universal and generally not serious has been borne out in self-report studies in several Western industrial countries (Farrington 1979; Frechette and Leblanc 1978; Williams and Gold 1972). As well, the notion of general delinquency has persisted in labelling theory, and forms the basis of the claim that society reacts to individuals and not to actions. The assumption of universality must not, however, ignore the fact that certain types of deviance, such as murder and sexual assault, are of considerable concern and importance to society. What is more important is that most acts of deviance, especially those committed by juveniles, are relatively inconsequential and transitory. Such a statement gains credibility when one realizes that most juveniles at one time or another violate drug and alcohol abuse laws and vandalism laws. In fact, in certain contexts such as high-school peer groups, types of norm-violating behaviour are outwardly condoned as acceptable. These reflections on the rather general nature of youth crime are presented with the discussion on selective policing to illustrate that, especially for non-serious types of crime, the decision to arrest is essentially discretionary.

Preferential Treatment and Counsel Status

The discretionary character of justice at the policing level seems to carry over into the court system (Matza 1964; Cicourel 1968; Platt 1969; Bala and

Corrado 1985). West (1984) and Thomas and Fitch (1981) have described the arbitrary and capricious nature of the North American youth court system, which, they argue, bases its decisions on both legal and extra legal concerns. The loose structure of the youth court system contributes to ambiguity of purpose and ambiguity of roles for social control agents. Erickson (1975) has investigated the perceptions and expectations of judges and social workers regarding private lawyers as compared to duty counsel. Expectations vary based on the type of counsel and the assumed incorrigibility of the offender, with private lawyers being granted a more adversarial posture in court proceedings. Dootjes, Erickson, and Fox (1972) have documented the actual impact on lawyers of these inarticulate perceptions. They suggest that the role confusion that lawyers experience results in a low commitment to the adversarial system and a rather passive stance regarding judicial decisions. Further research has argued that the posture taken by lawyers is partly the result of the philosophy of the particular court. Some courts are more inclined to permit adversarial procedures, while others depend on the conciliatory ability of court officials to deal with the 'problem' of the child rather than the legal elements of the case (Aday 1986).

The somewhat idiosyncratic nature of the youth court system is presented as a backdrop to the argument that counsel status partly determines judicial outcomes. Success in the adversarial system is based partly on the qualifications and competency of legal counsel. Wilkins (1976) and Wynne and Hartnagel (1975) in Canada and Blumberg (1979) and Heumann (1978) in the United States have shown that type of counsel directly affects judicial outcome, with private lawyers experiencing greater success than either legal aid or duty counsel in plea bargaining or trial procedures. The lawyer/client relationship is essentially a market relationship in which a lawyer's effort and his competency are based partly on remuneration; private lawyers are generally more expensive and more successful than duty counsel or legal aid lawyers (Brannigan 1984: 106-8). Ironically, though, Feld (1989) has argued that the actual presence of counsel may prejudice the court against the young offender, that American youth courts are more likely to show leniency to youth when the justice process is unencumbered by adversarial counsel.

Carrington and Moyer's recent research on the effects of legal representation on juvenile justice has illustrated the different 'styles' of youth courts across Canada (1990). Their findings suggest that counsel status effects vary across jurisdiction and that with few exceptions, counsel status has little impact on disposition, although in several jurisdictions counsel either mitigated dispositions (Montreal) or aggravated dispositions (Edmonton). The authors qualify these findings by suggesting that in an earlier research project (Carrington and Moyer 1990), the effect of counsel status on justice appeared at the adjudication stage. Here private lawyers were more successful than were duty counsel or public defenders in negotiating to have charges dropped or in defending not-guilty pleas.

Judicial Discretion in the Juvenile Justice System

Structure of Youth Court

It is evident from the previous discussion that class and race differentials exist at the initial stages of youth justice, at least in certain socio-cultural contexts. Such blatant biases invite the question, why our legal system is applied so unequally. The most obvious response is that law enforcers and legislators are permitted a great deal of discretionary power, and that, in general, social control agents maintain notions that lower-class and immigrant families are somehow deficient. The links between family structure, family ideology, and juvenile delinquency exist in family sociology of the structural-functionalist tradition; these same theoretical perceptions seem to persist throughout social control agencies.

While the existence of preferential treatment in adult court has received a considerable amount of research attention in North America, research on youth court has been sparse and somewhat contradictory in the United States, and virtually non-existent in Canada. The extant research has focused on the impact that legal versus extra-legal variables have on the treatment of offenders. Arguments range from those supporting the jurisprudential position that seriousness of offence and prior record are the primary considerations, to those endorsed by the conflict/labelling position that race, class, age, and gender are primary considerations in the administration of justice.

The argument that legal decisions are essentially formulated on the bases of the socio-cultural biases of social control agents appears in a body of literature that stresses the organization of law and the discretionary nature of the legal enterprise. Early observers stressed the unstructured nature of youth court (Matza 1964; Cicourel 1968; Platt 1969); later research has recognized that law enforcers and legislators endowed with a great deal of discretionary power render prejudicial assessments of lower-class, immigrant, and minority group families (Dootjes, Erickson, and Fox 1972; Erickson 1975). Hogarth's landmark study of the Canadian legal system has buttressed this body of research by suggesting the nature of the court and the nature of the judge as predisposing considerations in sentencing disparity (Hogarth 1971). Sentencing becomes a 'human process' when the magistrate is placed in the untenable position of having to make judgements in a system where roles and purposes are ambiguously defined. The 1980-1982 National Study on the Functioning of the Juvenile Court in Canada echoed Hogarth's conclusions that the variability of justice from court to court is typical of Youth Courts. The study revealed that variability amongst youth courts is based on locale, court philosophy, organizational structure, and the orientations of court officials. Doob and Beaulieu have recently argued that across Canada there is substantial variation among youth judges with respect to dispositions. They claim that the Young Offenders Act is partly responsible for this variation. The act ask judges to weigh many factors in arriving at dispositions; as a result, judges have an 'impossible task: combining sometimes contradictory goals to arrive at a disposition' (1993: 245). For a listing of the general goals of the Young Offenders Act to which judges are asked to respond, see Appendix I, sections 3 (1), (2), and (3), especially.

Thomas and Fitch (1981) have echoed the work of Hogarth (1971) and Doob and Beaulieu (1993)in their research into the American juvenile court system. They argue that no single factor is responsible for a judicial outcome. Instead they document the arbitrary and capricious nature of the system, and suggest that such a system necessarily results in decisions based on legal and extra-legal concerns. The juvenile system is described as one which must inevitably perpetuate discretion and preferential treatment. West (1984) has described the legal history of the North American juvenile court system: the system was originally constituted to be loosely articulated, explicitly for the purposes of maintaining judicial subjectivity—long considered the hallmark of the humanitarian, welfare approach to juvenile delinquency.

> The loose structure of the court, lack of due process, vague definitions of illegalities, and conflicting community pressures to 'crack down' or 'rehabilitate' force judges to rely on their commonsense (middle-class) notions of delinquency and its causal factors. They assess the 'situation' of the child . . . .(West 1984: 180)

It is important to reiterate that one of the primary considerations of the Young Offenders Act is to reduce the subjectivity of the court in an attempt to eliminate the arbitrary nature of youth justice. Although the current justice system maintains its child welfare mandate, its primary consideration is due process and impartial justice.

Family Power, Ethnicity, and Juvenile Justice

A second body of research has accepted the argument that the justice system is loosely organized, but has superimposed on it the more critical position that the social power of the defendant acts as a determinant of justice (Chambliss and Seidman 1971). Simply put, youths and their parents who have the socio-economic power to resist the administration of justice will be insulated from harsh justice. The mechanism is relatively uncomplicated. The parents of White, middle-class juveniles have a greater capacity to resist law enforcement. As Chambliss suggests:

> those people are arrested, tried, and sentenced who can offer the fewest rewards for nonenforcement of the laws and who can be processed without creating any undue strain for the organizations which comprise the legal system. (1969: 84)

At the arrest level, wealthier, more powerful parents can initiate false arrest cases and libel suits against the law enforcement agencies, a factor that may render the possibility of one of their children's arrest less likely. At the prosecution and disposition level, success in our adversarial judicial system is dependent in large part on the qualifications and capabilities of lawyers. Lower-class juveniles do not possess the informational or financial resources to obtain

efficient legal aid, nor do they have the resources to provide alternatives to incarceration, alternatives such as psychiatric or other professional help.

These arguments were supported by early research relating class and ethnicity with prosecution rates. Black juveniles were found to be prosecuted at rates from 15 to 30 per cent higher than middle-class White juveniles (Goldman 1963; Arnold 1971; Thornberry 1973). The same trends were found in the severity of judicial dispositions, again with lower-class and Black youths receiving harsher penalties (Ferdinand and Lechterhand 1970; Arnold 1971; Thornberry 1973). Thomas and Sieverdes (1975), comparing the impact of legal and extra-legal concerns in judicial decisions, found marginal import for the extra-legal variables such as race, family stability, sex, and the presence of a co-defendant. The impact of the latter group of concerns was markedly weaker than that of seriousness of offence and previous record. Marshall and Thomas (1983), who investigated discretionary decision making in juvenile court, analysed a rather complex legal and extra-legal model of court disposition and found support for the influence of age and ethnicity on judicial decisions. An important qualification in these studies was that the researchers controlled for level of delinquency involvement in order to eliminate the probability that arrests, prosecutions, and dispositions were simply a reflection of higher crime rates among lower-class and Black juveniles.

Both qualitative and quantitative research attempted to illustrate how financial and informational resources dictate success in an adversarial legal system. Langley, Thomas, and Parkinson (1978) studied the experiences of Ottawa juveniles in courtroom situations and illustrated a glaring absence of understanding and a vast discrepancy between youth expectations in terms of sentencing and actual sentences. Lack of understanding, involving ignorance of courtroom procedures and of parental responsibility, was evident in judicial proceedings. As a result, the authors noted, 'This lack of information, when coupled with moderate to high anxiety, or apprehensiveness on the part of youth, is a fertile breeding ground for a sense of injustice' (1978: 49). The low self-confidence of adolescents in an unfamiliar situation results in their taking deferential and servile postures, with the ultimate result an inordinately high rate of guilty pleas.

More recent studies have discussed the influence of family resources in combination with family structure as consideration in judicial decisions. Cruikshank (1981) has revealed problems encountered by Native families in northern Canadian environments, problems that disrupt the geographical and structural stability of the family. She suggests that rapid industrialization of Canada's northern frontier has created cultural disruption; one of the manifestations of this upheaval is the increasing incidence of matrifocal families, or at least families where the male is a temporary or sub-dominant member. Single-parent families face the dilemma of one person filling both support and nurturant roles, a situation which is compounded by the sexual and economic exploitation of Native women. Arguably, the problems stemming from cultural collision in places like the Yukon can be paralleled with problems arising when members of

Native families move from rural to urban environments in southern areas. The basic thrust of the argument involving matrifocality and delinquency is not that single-parent families are especially criminogenic, but rather that such families are generally seen as unacceptable by social control agents and are consequently dealt with prejudicially.

LaPrairie (1983), too, has presented data from a northern Canadian juvenile court and discusses the impact of family structures on success in the court system. LaPrairie illustrates the lack of success that Native juveniles experience in the court system relative to their non-Native counterparts, and how this discrepancy is related to the fact that a strong bias in favour of typical two-parent families exists amongst judicial agents. Fewer Native juveniles live with both parents than do non-Native juveniles, especially in Native communities in Northern Canada. These same Native juveniles are also assumed by police, judges, and court workers to be living in families described as having more problems than the families of non-Native juveniles. LaPrairie contends that juvenile courts tend to be biased in favour of intact families, and especially biased against single-parent, female-headed families.

It appears that conventional families, especially with the presence of a male guardian, present a more powerful, more threatening, front to the court system. Families in which the father is absent are not perceived as potentially threatening to the police, prosecutors, judges, and penal workers. These aspects—lack of power, accompanied by low economic resources—render juveniles from such families disadvantaged when confronted by social control agencies. This disadvantage is fostered and legitimated not only by the court system but also by the psychiatric profession, which has traditionally viewed the situation of children, and especially boys, living only with their mothers as a criminogenic situation (Donzelot 1979).

In light of these findings, it is the contention of this research that much like lower-class and Black youths in America, Native and Métis juveniles in Canada, and their families, do not have sufficient economic, legal, and educational resources to cope with an inflexible legal system, and consequently they are unfairly targeted for legal scrutiny.

Current quantitative research in the area of juvenile court justice answers the methodological and analytical criticisms that were levelled at earlier research on criminal courts (Hagan 1974). Relevant issues include the need to control for extra-legal and legal variables, to test the interaction effects between variables, and to analyse the juvenile justice system as a cumulative process (McCarthy and Smith 1986; Bishop and Frazier 1988). For example, Marshall and Thomas (1983) present a comprehensive analysis of decision-making in juvenile court. Their investigations on the legal and extra-legal influences on court decisions at successive stages of justice find support for the influences of age and ethnicity on judicial decisions. An important qualification in these studies is that the researchers have controlled for level of delinquency involvement in order to eliminate the probability that arrests, prosecutions, and dispositions simply reflect higher crime rates among lower-class and minority-group juveniles.

A current body of research on adult courts has underscored the necessity of specifying complete causal models (including extra-legal and legal variables, and court-specific variables such as geographic location), and the necessity of testing interaction effects between independent variables (Myers 1987, for example).

Thornberry (1979), Landau (1981), and Dannefer and Shutt (1982) test completely specified causal models of police and judicial discretion using log-linear analytic techniques. Their findings support the hypothesis that extra-legal concerns, especially race and class, have a strong influence on judicial decisions. Cohen and Kluegel (1979), however, use the same techniques in their analysis of intake screening decisions in juvenile courts in Memphis and Denver and show a strong influence of legal variables and no race or class bias, at least at the initial stages of the justice process. That legal variables are the primary determinants of juvenile outcome is supported by Bishop and Frazier (1988). However, the authors conclude that the relatively small influence of race at each stage of the justice process cannot be overlooked, given the cumulative effect of this phenomenon.

Similarly, McCarthy and Smith (1986) find that pre-trial detention and legal factors decline in importance as one moves through the judicial process, and that race increases in importance. Once again, the cumulative effects of extra-legal variables—especially the effect of race—is stressed. Furthermore, this effect is manifest at the later stages of the justice process. Finally, Feld (1989) has shown that American youth courts make decisions on the basis of social characteristics such as race and class and that, although access to legal counsel is a function of these characteristics, it is the resources of the family that ultimately dictate dispositions. As the authors argue, middle- and upper-class families are more likely than lower-class families to retain private counsel, but lenient justice results from family power and not counsel status (Feld 1989). The importance of racial/ethnic and class factors has been currently documented in the context of adult court, most notably by Myers (1987) and Zatz (1987) in the United States and in Canada by Mandel (1986) and Jackson (1989).

While studies such as the aforementioned are compelling, the readings of the evidence on the influence of extra-legal factors on prosecution and sentencing are somewhat mixed. Hagan (1974), Brantingham (1985), and Fox (1987) have all concluded that extra-legal factors are not significant in sentencing decisions (at any stage of the judicial process), and that prior record and pertinent legal facts are the most important considerations.

Justice for Native Juveniles

The relationship between race/ethnicity and justice is central to this research and, given the Canadian context, a major issue for this study is Aboriginal justice. Several Aboriginal justice inquiries have concluded recently that justice at all levels does not adequately serve Native Canadians (Manitoba Aboriginal Justice Inquiry, Alberta Justice Inquiry, etc. 1991). The injustices characteristic of the adult system are compounded in the youth system, which still holds to child welfare philosophies. I believe, as do many Native leaders in Canada, that impartial justice is not the norm for Aboriginal youth.

Some twenty-five years ago, Sebald (1968) discussed the plight of Native teenagers in the American juvenile system and suggested that anthropological studies had shown that Native teenagers were characterized by substantially different psychological structures than those of their non-Native counterparts. Some of these culturally determined psychological predispositions involved aspects of passive stoicism, interdependence, co-operation, and unemotional deportment. As admirable and as normal as these characteristics are, Sebald argued that North American judicial systems were premised on competition, aggression, and independence, and that the aforementioned values rendered Native teenagers relatively disadvantaged under judicial scrutiny. (For a detailed description of the collision between Native and legal culture, see Chapter Seven.)

A limited amount of research has documented the impact of race and class on juvenile justice in a Native Canadian context, and this research is primarily descriptive. Kueneman and Linden (1983) have shown the lack of success which Native juveniles encounter in Canada's legal system. In their study of a Winnipeg juvenile court, race (specifically, Native versus non-Native) was correlated with dispositions, although the influence of race was minor—when other relevant variables were controlled—as compared to the influences of prior record and seriousness of offence. LaPrairie and Griffiths (1982) have documented the over-representation of Native youth in court and have identified the socioeconomic characteristics that disadvantage Native youth relative to their non-Native peers. LaPrairie (1983) has further researched the experiences of Native youth in court and has suggested that the psychological disadvantage which Native juveniles bring into the court system is compounded by structural disadvantages. As LaPrairie has suggested,

> Because Native peoples in these communities [urban centres] have not acquired the prevailing standards of living that one might expect to accompany physical assimilation, they are subject to a system of justice that will judge their ability to be accountable and responsible on the basis of their social structure. (1983: 340)

This unenlightened demand for accountability should produce adverse results for Native juveniles at the prosecution and sentencing phases of the judicial process.

Hackler and Paranjape (1984) have combined an analysis of Canadian juvenile justice statistics with a review of American research on judicial discretion, and have hypothesized that 'the difference between Native and the Whites would be less at the beginning of the system than at the end' (1984: 196). In juvenile systems such as Alberta's and Manitoba's, which use the courts extensively in dealing with young offenders, the legal control of Native juveniles is especially severe. Hackler and Paranjape argue, however, that judges are not necessarily acting prejudicially against ethnicity and social class, but rather that they are reacting rationally to family situations characteristic of Native and lower-class juveniles. Rational judicial response, however, does not account for the generally unfounded link between ethnicity/social class and criminogenic families.

Boldt *et al.* (1983) have established that pre-sentence reports by probation officers have a strong influence on judges, and their research attempts to discern the factors which influence these reports, especially the factor of ethnicity. Their results reveal that prior record and seriousness of offence are the best predictors of recommendations for incarceration; Natives have high prior conviction records and also commit more serious crimes than non-Natives. The authors do, however, qualify these findings by suggesting that discriminatory justice may occur before probation recommendations through selective policing, and after probation recommendations, when access to competent legal help may determine avoidance of incarceration (Wynne and Hartnagel 1975; Klein 1976).

It bears repeating, at this point, that institutional judicial bias in Canada is compounded by racial discrimination at the arrest level—I have discussed policing bias in an earlier section in this chapter. The works of Hylton (1981) on juvenile arrest and Ericson (1982) and Shearing (1981) on adult arrest alert us to the significance of policing discretion, as well as judicial discretion, on discriminatory youth justice.

Universality of Delinquent Behaviour

The statement that delinquency is universal and generally not serious is of considerable importance to the arguments presented in this book. The historical significance of such a position is shown in Chapter Two in which I discuss how, throughout Canada's post-industrial revolution history, common and innocuous acts of delinquency when committed by marginal and underclass children were deemed to be serious enough for state intervention. A basic premise of the theoretical position of this work is that, while most juveniles commit crime, certain categories of youth are more closely watched, more often arrested, and more severely punished by the legal system than are other categories of young offenders. Youth crime rates, then, are as much a function of those who are caught as those who have done wrong. And, of course, the justice system is positioned against those whose culture is most unlike the culture of the law. (See Chapter Seven.)

The universal nature of youth crime has been borne out in self-report studies in several Western industrial countries. While self-report methodologies are not perfect in their estimations of youth misconduct, they do give us a clearer sense not only of the extent of actual crime committed, but also of the relationship between crime committed and crime detected. As we can see from the following studies, youth misconduct is widespread and generally not serious.

Elmhorn (quoted in Corrado, LeBlanc, and Trepanier 1983: 33) reported a 93 per cent delinquency rate in Sweden in 1965; Williams and Gold indicated a rate of 88 per cent in a national sample for ages 13-16 in the United States in 1972;

and Farrington revealed that 96 per cent of his sample of working-class adolescents in England report delinquency involvement in 1979. More recent studies, including the Elliot and Ageton study (1980) based on the National Youth Survey in the United States, indicate quite clearly that youth crime misconduct is widespread and that most violations go undetected. Elliot and Ageton contend that 84 per cent of all young offenders are never arrested and that arrest patterns are not representative of all offenders but represent a bias in terms of race, class, and gender. This argument forms the central thesis informing the empirical analysis here.

In Canada, Frechette and Leblanc (1978) determined that 92.8 per cent of adolescents between the ages of 12 and 18 had committed one deviant act, and 81.8 per cent had contravened the criminal code. LeBlanc's own work (1983) is noteworthy in a Canadian context for its methodological rigour and for the longitudinal nature of the study. For a period of five years, LeBlanc studied a random sample of 3,000 Montreal youths. His findings revealed that over the course of a year, over 90 per cent of all youths sampled had committed crimes that, if the law had been strictly applied, would have brought them before youth courts. LeBlanc attributed the common occurrence of youth misconduct to the process of learning by testing the boundaries of acceptable conduct. This interpretation suggests that all groups of youths are equally likely to engage in crime, and despite whether this is normal or abnormal conduct, the reality is that very few of these crimes are serious (between 8 and 10 per cent of all youth crime), and most youth crimes are transitory (LeBlanc 1983). How, then, do we explain the fact that some young offenders continue in a career of crime and others find their way into more conventional activities? The explanations are complex, but one argument is that the selective application of the law at one stage or another of the justice process contributes in part to the evolution of young offenders into career criminals.

Labelling theory is instructive in attempting to explain how discriminatory justice is criminogenic. From this perspective, inconsequential types of behaviour become important only when the violator is isolated for punishment and public degradation. Such treatment may devastate the individual's self-concept, 'altering the psychic structure, producing specialized organization of social roles and self-regarding attitudes' (Lemert 1967). Given that a major premise of a labelling theory approach to criminogenesis is that social control agencies, through the processes of isolation and publication, produce given rates of crime, I would argue that agencies like the police and the judiciary, responding preferentially towards certain categories of juveniles and prejudicially towards others (Thornberry 1979; Landau 1981; Dannefer and Shutt 1982), may inadvertently foster youth criminality.

In addressing the issue of deviance as a social definition, labelling theory is partly concerned with the use and abuse of power in the creation of categories of abnormal behaviour. However, an equally important concern is the psychological effect of being labelled a norm violator. With regard to juvenile delinquency, the macro-social underpinnings of labelling theory locate the existing structural inequalities in the policing institutions and the judicial system. The social-psychological dimension of labelling theory is concerned with the impact of the exposure to the crime control system on the offender's psychological structure. Exposure to social control agencies may erode social status and restrict education and employment opportunities, and may result in continued close scrutiny by law-enforcement personnel. The social stigma and lack of privilege resulting from such labelling may then result in the internalization of a negative self-concept and the offender's acceptance of society's evaluations.

Labelling as an evolutionary process is best depicted by Lemert (1967) in his theoretical model, which posits that primary deviant acts or initial rule-breaking actions arise from diverse cultural and social contexts, and as such, are transitory. However, the act gains importance when the social response to the unsanctified act influences an individual's psychological make-up. Certain individuals tend to view themselves as others see them, and their personalities and behaviours are reorganized on the basis of public definitions. This redefinition of self may result in behaviour that is persistently deviant and is thus consistent with the social stigma. Such a profile constitutes, for Lemert, a 'secondary deviant'. Suffice it to say, at this point, that from Lemert's labelling perspective, delinquency is the result of an individual's exposure to public scrutiny and the resulting redefinition of self which such scrutiny determines.

The preoccupation with the development of deviant identities has been one of the major criticisms of labelling theory especially in its application to juvenile delinquency. Critics have suggested that by focusing on the period between the initial act of deviance and the final stage of acceptance of the deviant label, prior considerations such as biological predispositions and family socialization are ignored. The theory is indicted for disregarding the motivations behind primary deviant acts and for placing the blame primarily on the shoulders of social injustice.

The notion of the universality of rule-breaking behaviour has persisted in labelling theory over time; in essence labelling claims that society reacts to individuals and not to actions. As mentioned previously, the claim that delinquent behaviour is universal does not mean that all acts of youth crime are inconsequential. Non-serious types of violations, however, constitute the majority of youth crime, and these violations—and the selective arrest and punishment of them—form the focus of the present study.

Although the psychological process of labelling presents an important and compelling argument when discussing juvenile justice, it is not tested in this research. The merits of such an approach are in the author's opinion, borne out by previous psychological and interactionist research, and are well-documented and defensible. I have discussed labelling in the context of this study because it presents an important paradigm for extended research in the area of institutional labelling and youth misconduct. Furthermore, many of the basic principles of the Young Offenders Act are based on issues raised by labelling theorists, including provisions of confidentiality and diversion (see YOA sections 4 and 38 in Appendix I for the specific provisions). Confidentiality of young offenders' records, prohibition of the publishing of names, and diversion and alternative measures are strategies all intended to avoid the legal stigmatization of young offenders. It is the initial stigma or label that labelling theorists envision as the starting point of a career in crime for many young offenders.

The investigation of the nature of juvenile justice in this book is an attempt to test whether justice is a process based on advantage, the implication being that such a process nurtures the internalization of delinquent self-concept for the disadvantaged. In summary, it is disparate treatment which lies at the heart of individual internalization of deviant labels, and in order to defend such a view of criminogenesis, it is necessary first to document the existence of discriminatory application of the law.

The Young Offenders Act

The Young Offenders Act was implemented to redress the ambiguity and unfairness that was inherent in the Juvenile Delinquency Act—specifically, to address the problems surrounding the widespread use of informality, the lack of due process, and the uncertainty surrounding age and penalty guidelines. Simply put, juvenile court reform was necessary given the widespread view that the Juvenile Delinquency Act had failed. In the spirit of the new act, implemented in 1985, young offenders were to have universal access to the adversarial system, including competent counsel and provisions for alternative measures to incarceration. As well, the trivial acts of deviance (status offences), which were covered by the Juvenile Delinquency Act, were no longer under the purview of the youth court. In essence, the new act was to meld the best of the due process model of justice—which was characteristic of the adult system—with the child welfare model—which was retained from the former juvenile court system.

A substantial body of literature exists which describes the aftershocks of the Young Offenders Act. The overall theme in this literature is that the welfare model has not been sustained and that a crime control agenda lurks beneath the rhetoric of liberal reform and due process (Caputo and Bracken 1988). Leschied and Jaffe (1987), for example, have argued that deterrence through punishment is becoming more commonplace in youth courts since the inception of the act, and that rehabilitation is being abandoned in lieu of formal and restrictive procedures. Markwart and Corrado (1989) show that since the Young Offenders Act, courts in several provincial jurisdictions have been characterized by substantial increases in open and closed custody dispositions. Further, Doob (1993) qualifies these claims by suggesting that, indeed, custodial dispositions have increased since the Young Offenders Act, but the average length of sentence has decreased overall. In addition, the number of relatively long sentences has diminished. It is ironic that this increasingly punitive system of youth justice (marked by a series of amendments in 1986 and 1989 to toughen the Young Offenders Act) is still being criticized by crime control advocates and citizen lobbies as being too lenient with young offenders. Caputo (1991), by placing the Young Offenders Act in historical context, has shown that the *de facto* development of a more punitive system of control of young offenders was consistent with the neo-conservative tenor of the 1980s. Such historical work favours the predominant theme of research on the Young Offenders Act: despite liberal reformist rhetoric, coercive crime control strategies prevail in juvenile justice in Canada.

This brief discussion of the Young Offenders Act is important given that the data used in this study were acquired shortly after the act was implemented. Consequently, the results need to be considered in the context of a newly reformed justice system that is both more uncertain and more formalized than in the past. The implications for this research are twofold. Firstly, it appears that the courts are more willing since the Young Offenders Act than before to process young offenders formally and to use the full authority of the law in meting out punishment. Secondly, the adversarial system, at least in principle, appears to be the mechanism through which the state claims due process for young offenders. My research needs to be considered in this new legal context, which advocates due process as empowering for accused young offenders.

chapter five

Analytical Models of Youth Justice

This chapter offers a research design testing the major issues presented in the previous chapters. The models used in this analysis of the juvenile justice system are presented in a sequence which reflects the chronological order of the justice process. The first model predicts type of offence and represents the arrest or policing stage. Models two through five include decision to detain or release upon arrest, counsel type, plea, and adjudication. The final model predicts sentencing (disposition), the last stage of the judicial process in this analysis. Such a sequential analysis is used as a technique of specification to test, for example, whether extra-legal variables such as age and sex, which are significant at the first stage, influence legal discretion further along in the judicial process. In all of the proposed models, race remains the focal explanatory (causal) variable of interest. The relationships between race and judicial outcomes constitute the primary hypothesis in each stage. Explanations of the variables for the following models can be found in the section entitled *Methodology* (page 73).

Stages of Youth Justice

Seriousness of Offence

The seriousness of offence variable is based on the type of offence for which the charge is made. The type of offence is divided into serious versus non-serious crime on the basis of the criminal code and civic statutes. It would be reckless to suggest that police discretion and bias alone are at work at the charge stage. It is likely that police decisions to charge individuals for committing crimes are partially based on solid evidence that an actual crime has been committed. I have, however, indicated that discretion does occur prior to this, at the decision to arrest level (Piliavin and Briar 1964; Cicourel 1968; Landau 1981). It would be equally inaccurate, therefore, to suggest that a model predicting commission of juvenile crime, on the basis of court data, indicates actual crime committed. It must be remembered that arrest is an indication only of crime detected. Therefore, in stage one, with respect to seriousness of crime, police discretion is involved in arrest, but such discretion is not susceptible to direct measurement.

The major hypothesis tested in this model involves the influence of race on seriousness of offence. The other relevant variables that impact on seriousness of offence include sex, age, and previous conviction. Attendant hypotheses would suggest that males commit more serious crimes than females, that older juveniles are also more likely to commit serious offences (Hepburn 1978; Landau 1981), and that previous conviction strongly influences crime committed. These hypotheses test the work of Boldt *et al.* (1983), which finds that Natives are charged for committing more serious crimes than non-Natives, and that they have higher prior conviction rates. A logit model predicting seriousness of offence by race, age, sex, and previous conviction is used to test the hypotheses.

Pre-Appearance Status—Detention on Arrest

The model predicting pre-appearance status is essentially a model which tests a certain element of police and judicial discretion. The assessment by the police and judicial authorities as to whether an individual is a danger to society or whether such an individual is responsible enough to appear on his or her own accord, should be the basis of the decision to detain or to summon (see section 7, YOA, Appendix I) . According to the Canadian ideal of justice, decisions should be made primarily on the bases of seriousness of crime and an individual's record, and not on the basis of extra-legal concerns. If, however, race is related to decisions to detain on arrest when legal variables are accounted for, discriminatory justice is being practised. McCarthy and Smith (1986) and Bishop and Frazier (1988) argue that decisions to detain on arrest are not discriminatory, but they offer the suggestion that detention on arrest becomes an important influence on decisions further on in the process.

Again, the major hypothesis in the present study tests the influence of race on judgements to detain on arrest or summon. A five-way contingency model is used to test in logit form the main and interaction effects of race, age, sex, and previous conviction on pre-appearance status. A second model substitutes seriousness of offence for previous conviction. The limitations of the relatively small sample size prevent inclusion of previous conviction and seriousness of offence in a single six-way contingency table.

Counsel Status

As suggested previously, success in an adversarial judicial system is based partly on access to counsel, and access to counsel is determined by socio-economic status (Chambliss 1969; Erickson 1975). The Young Offenders Act has ensured that some type of representation is mandatory for an accused youth (see sections 11 and 12, Appendix I). The logit models predicting counsel status analyse those legal and extra-legal characteristics that determine type of counsel, specifically the influences of race and the combined influences of race, age, sex, seriousness of offence, and record. The methodological definition of the counsel status variable is explained in the section entitled *Variable Description* (page 74). Counsel status is subsequently entered into models predicting plea and disposition.

Plea

The next step in the formal judicial process, after initial appearance, involves the entering of a plea. The plea variable in this study involves only those cases in which it was necessary for the defendant to enter a plea; as a consequence, private lawyers or duty counsel were present in all of the cases. The appearances where some type of representation was not present were adjourned in order for the accused to obtain duty counsel.

As in previous models, the main relationship of interest is that between race and plea; the relative impact of race is assessed against the influences of seriousness of offence and counsel status. As Langley, Thomas, and Parkinson (1978) suggest, the decision to plead guilty is not determined exclusively by legal considerations, such as crime committed, but also by counsel support and advice and offender familiarity with the legal system. Family support is also included in these models predicting pleas.

I have noted previously that judicial officials react to the presence or absence of family support. The model presented here proposes that family support impacts at an earlier stage, in the determination of the decision to plead guilty and forego challenging the system or to plead not guilty and face an adversarial procedure. Lack of sophistication and inexperience with legal procedure may place juveniles at a distinct disadvantage in a technical, bureaucratic, judicial system. I attempt to test this proposition by evaluating previous conviction (indicating previous contact with the law) as an explanatory variable in determination of plea. Such a model should shed light on whether those individuals with previous convictions have access to private counsel or legal aid more so than first offenders, and whether, having been through the judicial process, they are more familiar with the conventions characteristic of the system. As in the previous model, race, family presence and counsel status are included in the analysis.

The variable 'plea' is an important factor in the conceptual scheme explaining judicial process. The act of pleading guilty or not guilty is partially the result of an individual's willingness to confront the judicial system and fight back, to take a nonfatalistic posture towards his/her own future. A plea represents not so much an idiosyncrasy of the system, but rather a variation in an offender's willingness to take a proactive rather than a reactive stance towards jurisprudence. The Young Offenders Act has provided the legal context in which proactive justice is ensured: see YOA section 3 (1) (e).

It would be preferable, methodologically and conceptually, to include race, counsel status, record, family presence, and seriousness of offence in one complete logit model. Unfortunately, the sample size for these data prohibits me from generating one complete six-way contingency table. As a consequence, I have chosen the two aforementioned models as a substitute for the preferred six-way model. Seriousness of offence and record have been separated in previous analyses. This analysis is consistent with those previous tests and is justified on the same premises, with the same caveat that my models are vulnerable to possible specification error.

Adjudication

Court decisions to convict or to withdraw charges have been shown to be based on legal concerns such as evidence and seriousness of offence, and partly on advice from the prosecution and court workers. It has also been suggested that such judgements are made on more arbitrary bases and include influences such as offender's race and the presence of private counsel. For this study, information as to whether the crime was actually committed is obviously not available. Therefore, one of the possible flaws in a model predicting conviction is that guilt or innocence, based on actual crime committed, is indeterminable. This puts the study in the untenable position of assessing guilt or innocence outcomes on the basis of court-specific concerns rather than evidence. Nonetheless, I am concerned with the relative influences of seriousness of offence, counsel status, and race as determinants of conviction, rather than the absolute causes of conviction outcomes.

Disposition

The last model to be tested in this analysis predicts sentence/disposition, the final stage in the judicial process. Based on the same conceptual and methodological reasoning presented in the previous section, the impact of criminal record on sentencing is tested separately from that of seriousness of offence. As Chambliss (1969) and Langley *et al.* (1978) have suggested, access to counsel and the ability to afford private lawyers have a determinant influence on judicial decisions, especially at the disposition phase. In a similar vein, LaPrairie (1983), Cruikshank (1981), and Hackler and Paranjape (1984) have discussed the possibility that courts react to family situations which they typify on the bases of race and class.

Two models test the aforementioned influences of family and counsel on disposition. I analyse the main and interaction effects of race and criminal record with counsel and family, and then test the same model, substituting seriousness of offence for criminal record. Boldt *et al.* (1983) have suggested that prior record and seriousness of offence are the best predictors of sentencing, and that Natives have higher rates of prior record and commit more serious crimes; these associations explain the race effect. The two models predicting disposition test the hypotheses that race, counsel status, and family presence have unique influences on disposition when seriousness of offence and record are controlled for. In general, these models test the claim of Hackler and Paranjape (1984) that in juvenile systems such as Alberta's, the selection of Native juveniles is inordinately severe.

Methodology

Data for this research were collected by the John Howard Society of Alberta. For a ten-week period beginning 20 May 1986 and ending 25 July 1986, direct observations were made on every appearance in Edmonton Youth Court. The youth court was composed of three individual courtrooms: one docket court, which handled primarily first appearances and nontrial matters, and two trial courts. A team of observers comprised of three university students and a research staff coordinator gathered legal and extra-legal data on 1,582 individuals appearing in court.

Recordings of extra-legal, and court-specific variables were made on the basis of direct observation. Legal variables such as type of offence, number of appearances, and trial status were taken directly from court docket sheets. These data were recorded on a predetermined coding sheet, a sample of which can be found in Appendix II. The extra-legal variables included sex, age, and race. The age variable was determined only in approximately half of the cases. However, the researchers cross-tabulated the sex and the number of offences for the unknown category of individuals and found them to be almost identical to the known category. The race variable was recorded on the basis of categories of 'White', 'Native', and 'Other'. The legal variables include 'type of offence', 'pre-appearance status', 'number of offences', 'previous conviction', 'plea entered', 'adjudication', and 'type of disposition'. The court-specific variables involve 'presence of parent or guardian' and 'type of representation'. The actual categories for these variables are described in the following section.

It is important to note that previous conviction and seriousness of offence could be determined in approximately 50 per cent of the cases. While these variables are central to accurate estimates of extra-legal effects, I have no reason to believe that the data were selected for any systematic reason. Although it is regrettable that the sample size is diminished, I am confident that no systematic error has been introduced by the missing cases.

The original purpose of the John Howard Society study was to acquire a descriptive analysis of the Edmonton Youth Court, including a legal and extra-legal aggregate profile of young offenders in a specified ten-week time period. The data are adequate, however, to justify more sophisticated inferential analyses. I have used basic log-linear analytic techniques to test models based on research discussed earlier in the problems section. Because I wish to posit these models as unidirectional causal models, I use the logit format of log-linear analysis (Gilbert 1981; Knoke and Burke 1986). Essentially, this type of analysis permits assessments regarding the relative impact of specified independent variables on a dependent variable, using odds ratios. The major benefit of the technique is that magnitude of the effect of one variable on another can be determined while controlling for a series of other relevant factors. The mechanics of the analysis are explained in the results for Table 6.1.

The models presented earlier are tested on the basis of four-way and five-way contingency tables. To facilitate interpretation and the avoidance of empty cells, most variables have been collapsed into dichotomies. Collapsing is based partly on theoretical concerns and partly on the technique described in Knoke and Burke (1986). When dummy or effect-coded categories show little or no difference from other categories, they are combined with their similar categories. An illustration of this technique appears in the following section describing the collapsing of categories.

Variable Description

Legal Variables

In the John Howard survey, the 'type of offence' variable was classified into offence categories coded according to the Canadian Criminal Code, provincial statutes, and Edmonton civic ordinances. 'Type of offence' is a major predictor variable in all the prospective logit models of this study, and to facilitate entry into these models, 'type of offence' has been collapsed into two categories represented by a serious/non-serious dichotomy. The initial categories have been collapsed into a ten-category scale of 'type of crime', proposed by Sellin and Wolfgang (1964: 145-64), which basically categorizes crimes on the basis of victimization and property loss. These ten categories are further collapsed into a dichotomy which separates violations into serious (involving third-party harm) and non-serious (generally considered offences subject to summary procedures, which are based on simplified procedural rules with limited fact-finding or discovery). Two categories in the Sellin and Wolfgang scale, property theft and property damage, contain both indictable and summary types of offences; such ambiguous within-category offences are individually recoded into the appropriate serious/non-serious category.

'Pre-appearance' status describes whether an offender has been detained or summoned prior to appearing in court, and suggests a discretionary policing decision based on assumptions regarding danger to society and responsibility for appearing in court.

The initial 'counsel status' variable identifies young offenders who are represented by private lawyers or legal aid (45%), by duty counsel (24.5%), by another adult (often Native Counselling Services, 2.5%), and those with no representation (28%). The cases with no representation are generally adjourned in order to have the offender consult with duty counsel. So for this analysis, the counsel status variable is dichotomized into 'non-duty counsel' (private lawyer or legal aide) and 'duty counsel' (duty counsel and other). The 'number of offences' variable is dichotomized into single offence (61.8%) and multiple offence (more than one, 38.2%). The presence of a parent or a significant other in court (including legal guardian, close relative, or a member of Native Counselling Services) was originally determined from direct observation. The attendant variable in the present model is dichotomized to indicate those cases where a parent or significant other was present in court (57.9%) and where the offender was unaccompanied (42.1%). Criminal record, determined in only 748 of 1,583 cases, is indicated by previous conviction (65.4%) versus no previous conviction (34.6%).

For those appearances in which the young person entered a plea (N = 1,367), 43% pleaded guilty, 40% reserved plea, and 17% pleaded not guilty. For the purpose of entering plea in a prediction model, only those court appearances where an actual guilty or not-guilty plea was entered have been selected.

The 'adjudication' variable is dichotomized into convicted versus withdrawal of charges. Eighty-five per cent of the cases adjudicated resulted in convictions. This skewed distribution presents somewhat of a problem for logit analysis. However, I have restricted the analysis to a four-way contingency model, including race, seriousness of offence, and counsel status, variables which are theoretically relevant to judicial decisions (Chambliss 1969). For those individuals who were convicted, dispositions were recorded into ten categories, including probation, types of restitution (community service, repayment), fines, and open and closed custody. (For a detailed list of the types of disposition available under the Young Offenders Act, see section 20, Appendix I.) The 'disposition' variable is dichotomized into two categories identifying those offenders who were punished and exposed to no further accountability or scrutiny (fine, discharge, compensation) and those whose punishment involved continued surveillance (probation, community service) or incarceration. As labelling theory suggests, continuous scrutiny by social control agencies has an important influence on the development of a criminal orientation, so the 'disposition' variable is designed to tap this influence.

Extra-Legal Variables

During the original research, the sex of the offender was determined from observation as being 83.5% males and 16.5% females. The distribution is quite similar to the 1985 Solicitor General of Alberta statistics comparing number of offenders charged by sex: 81.3% male and 18.7% female. Age was recorded in only half the appearances. However, when the cases in which age is unknown are compared with cases in which age is known on the bases of sex and number of offences, the distributions of sex and number of offences are similar. Further, the John Howard Society compared its findings to 1983 juvenile offender age distributions for Manitoba and found distributions of sex and number of offences to be similar—Manitoba statistics were used instead of Solicitor General of Alberta statistics because the Alberta government statistics do not break down juvenile offence by age; moreover, the comparison indicated inter-provincial similarity among juvenile offender statistics.

The variable 'age' has been dichotomized into categories grouping ages 12 to 15 and 16 to 18 to facilitate entry in the logit analysis. This break point is used partly on the grounds that 16 is the age of legal responsibility, and the legal age dividing children from adults in most jurisdictions. Also, the age variable is subjected to the Knoke and Burke (1986) technique in which age categories are included in a model predicting seriousness of crime; the results indicate that age categories 12, 13, 14, 15 exhibit little difference among age groups with respect to the effects of age on seriousness of crime. The same phenomenon is found for the categories 16, 17, and 18. Unfortunately, age was recorded in only about half of the appearances, reducing cell counts for a contingency table analysis. Such a limitation does reduce my ability to analyse higher-level contingency tables, and has forced me to separate certain prediction models into two five-way tables instead of one six-way table.

'Race' is an important predictor variable in all of the forthcoming analyses. Recording race can be quite subjective, and in an attempt to reduce error, race has been categorized into White (73%), Native (18%), and Other (encompassing non-White, non-Native ethnic groups, 9%). The frequencies for all the variables used in this analysis are presented in tabular form in Appendix II. The sample sizes for each analysis are somewhat different from the sample sizes in this table due to listwise deletion of missing cases. Chapter Six presents the results of the analysis described herein.

chapter six

Youth Court Analysis

The results of the youth-court data are analysed using a technique called logistic regression, described in the previous chapter. The technique is appropriate especially for legal data because most of these data are in non-numeric (nominal-level) form. The logit form of logistic regression uses the common-sense notion of 'odds' to explain the likelihood of an occurrence such as 'plea of guilty' given that other variables are present such as 'being Native' and 'being female'. Moreover, the technique allows the analyst to discuss the somewhat complicated interactions that occur between variables like race and gender, and the impact that the terms, either in isolation or in interaction with one another, have on outcomes like plea and sentencing.

Although the technical language of this analysis is somewhat confusing, the basic premises of the analysis are relatively straightforward. Firstly, it is important that we understand that with each analysis, the variable under consideration is the dependent variable; our concern, then, is in trying to establish what causes changes in that variable. Secondly, with each analysis, different combinations (models) of causal (independent) variables occur; the techniques for choosing the model that best explains the relationship between the dependent variable and the combinations of independent variables are described below. Thirdly, the odds ratios that are used to judge causal influences are best viewed as relative measures rather than absolute values. For example, when I use a specific odds ratio such as -.585, the important considerations are the negative sign that indicates a smaller chance of occurrence for that category of individual relative to the category omitted, and the magnitude of the coefficient relative to other coefficients within the same model. The omitted category to which I refer is the category not represented in the table, but explained in the Note at the bottom of each table. The following passage describes, in technical terms, how the judgements are made regarding the most appropriate combinations of causal variables.

The baseline model, Column 1, indicates the total chi-square to be accounted for by the subsequent models. The coefficient of determination (1-L_i^2/L_i^2) is calculated on this baseline model and is interpreted as a proportion of total chi-square explained by the model. The probability corresponding to each chi-square provides a basis for judging at which point the chi-square (L^2) indicates a highly probable correspondence between observed and predicted values of the cells in the table. When these observed and predicted values are similar, the probability level of the chi-square will depart from zero (ideally greater than .05). At this point, the model that demonstrates the correspondence is the model that most accurately fits the empirical data and which best explains the relationships between extra-legal and legal variables (in the real world). In selecting a preferred model the following criteria are considered: (a) the size of the chi-square (L^2) relative to the baseline chi-square (represented by the coefficient of determination (1-L_i^2/L_j^2); (b) the probability level corresponding to the chi-square (probabilities of greater than .05 are determined to represent models which accurately predict observed cell means); and (c), the presence or absence of significant log odds coefficients in the selected model.

Seriousness of Crime

Table 6.1 presents the logit analysis for the initial model predicting seriousness of crime committed by race, age, sex, and criminal record.

The chi-square statistics for this table reveal that Column 5 is the first model to achieve significance, indicating an excellent fit of the expected to the observed cell counts. The coefficient of determination shows that 75% of the baseline chi-square is explained by this model. The twelve two-way interaction terms explain 58% more of the chi-square than do the main effects of race, age, sex, and criminal record. As well, the introduction of interactions between previous conviction and age, previous conviction and sex, and age and sex, account for 19% more of this baseline chi-square than Model 4, which includes only two-way interactions with race. In Model 6, the introduction of all three-way interactions with race explains 24% more of the baseline chi-square than does Model 5; however, none of these terms is statistically significant.

From the preferred model, Model 5, the main effects of race suggest initially that the odds of White offenders being arrested for serious crimes (.548) are greater than the odds for Natives and substantially greater than for Others. For Others, those who are neither Native nor White, the likelihood of being arrested for serious offences (-.866) is significantly less than for Natives or Whites. However, the effect of race on seriousness of offence is more complicated than these findings suggest. When we observe the interaction terms between categories of race and age, race and criminal record, and criminal record and sex in Model 5, we see that the influences of legal and extra-legal variables on justice are complex, and that making sense of this complexity is difficult but necessary.

The first set of interaction terms suggest that the greater arrest rates for White offenders applies only to the younger (12-15 years) age category in which the log odds of being arrested for serious crimes (.490) are greater than for Natives or Others, while for the race category of Other in the same age grouping, the chances of arrest for serious offences are substantially less (–.718) than for Natives and Whites. In fact, sixteen- to eighteen-year-old White offenders are less likely to commit and be charged with serious crimes than are Native or Other sixteen- to eighteen-year-olds.

The interaction terms between race and criminal record (preconviction) suggest that for Native offenders with previous conviction records, the log odds of falling into the serious crime category are lower (–.645) than for the entire group of juveniles, while Native first-offenders stand a greater chance of being arrested for serious crimes than do White or Other first-offenders. Other first-offenders then have a less than average chance of appearing for serious crimes. The influence of record on seriousness of offence is not apparent for White offenders.

The last significant interaction term in Model 5, previous conviction by male, suggests that males with records are more likely to be arrested for serious crimes

Table 6.1 Logit Models of Arrest for Serious Crime by Race, Age, Sex, and Criminal Record (N = 484)

PREDETERMINED VARIABLES	MODEL					
	(1) BASELINE	(2) RACE MAIN EFFECT	(3) ALL MAIN EFFECTS	(4) 2-WAY RACE INTER-ACTION	(5) ALL 2-WAY INTER-ACTION	(6) 3-WAY RACE INTER-ACTION
MAIN EFFECTS						
Constant	1.314*	1.155*	1.239*	1.051*	1.187*	1.266*
Race						
White		.290**	.298**	.604*	.548*	.424
Native		–.099	–.138	.323	.318	.421
Other		–.191	–.160	–.927*	–.866*	–.845
Age						
12-15			.210*	–.110	–.025	.060
Record, Precon						
(Preconviction)			–.001	–.054	–.400**	–.831**
Sex						
Male			–.030	.260	.102	.012

Table 6.1 (continued)

	MODEL					
	(1)	(2)	(3)	(4)	(5)	(6)
PREDETERMINED		RACE	ALL	2-WAY RACE	ALL 2-WAY	3-WAY RACE
VARIABLES	BASELINE	MAIN	MAIN	INTER-	INTER-	INTER-
		EFFECT	EFFECTS	ACTION	ACTION	ACTION
INTERACTION EFFECTS						
12-15 by White				.515*	.490*	.267
12-15 by Native				.180	.228	.916
12-15 by Other				−.695*	−.718*	−1.183
Precon by White				.060	−.007	.489
Precon by Native				−.713*	−.645*	−.972
Precon by Other				.653*	.652*	.483
Male by White				−.383	−.295	−.081
Male by Native				−.127	−.210	−.329
Male by Other				.510	.505	.410
Precon by 12-15					−.195	−.077
Precon by Male					.446*	.910**
12-15 by Male					−.015	−.217
White, 12-15, Precon						−.243
Native, 12-15, Precon						.254
Other, 12-15, Precon						−.011
White, Male, Precon						−.631
Native, Male, Precon						.349
Other, Male, Precon						.282
White, 12-15, Male						.464
Native, 12-15, Male						−1.018
Other, 12-15, Male						.554
L^2	43.63	40.52	36.36	19.31	11.00	.29
d.f.	23	21	18	12	9	3
prob.	.005	.005	.005	.075	.250	.975
$1-L_i^2/L_j^2$		.071	.167	.557	.748	.993

NOTE: All coefficients are parameters of the additive logit model and are maximum-likelihood estimates calculated using glim (Baker and Nelder 1978). The dichotomous variables are categorized as follows: Seriousness of Crime, serious vs non-serious; Age, 12-15 vs 16-18; Record, previous conviction (precon) vs no precon; Sex, male vs female. The variable race is trichotomized into White, Native, and Other.

*Estimate significant at alpha = .05
**Estimate significant at alpha = .10

than are first-offenders, a finding which is expected. However, female repeat-offenders are less likely than first-offenders to fall into the serious crime category, the implication being that for females, having been previously convicted engenders a hesitancy to commit serious crime or a hesitancy on the part of the police to arrest female offenders. These findings partially support the findings of Hepburn (1978) and Gagnon and Biron (1979) that males commit more violent types of crime than do females. However, in my research, I have found that the greater male to female relationship holds only for repeat-offenders. For first-offenders, it appears that the corollary is the case, with females committing and being arrested for more serious types of crime. It is defensible that specific deterrence influences female juvenile conduct, while the same deterrence effect is not present for males. It is equally possible that the police tend to arrest females only for serious crimes, while they tend to arrest males for both serious and non-serious types of offences.

The chance of being arrested for a crime results from actual crime committed as well as from police decisions to arrest. I have argued previously that juvenile delinquent conduct is almost universal and that crime committed varies little across race, class, and education, especially for non-serious crimes. It is defensible, then, that the seriousness variable results, at least in part, from police discretion. Despite the difficulty in determining whether seriousness of crime results from actual crime committed or from this police discretion, it is nonetheless possible to draw some general conclusions from the previous five-way logit model. First, as previous research has indicated, sex and age do affect seriousness of offence. However, it appears that these influences vary across categories of race and criminal record. In general, age does not influence the seriousness of the offence for Native offenders, but does for White and Other offenders. For the Others only, an increase in age seems to dictate a greater likelihood of being arrested for serious crime. Sex appears to have an influence on seriousness of crime in concert with previous conviction. Male first-offenders are arrested for serious crimes proportionately less often than are female first-offenders. To reiterate, the contention that males commit and are arrested for more serious crimes than are females holds only for the category of repeat-offenders. Finally, criminal record has a decisive influence on seriousness of offence in interaction with race: Native first-offenders are arrested for serious crimes more often than Whites or Others. As a corollary, Native juveniles who are repeat-offenders are less likely than average to be charged with serious crimes, while Other juveniles with previous convictions are more likely to be charged with such crimes. These findings, then, tell us about the nature of police arrests; record, age, and gender are taken into account upon arrest, but these influences vary depending on the race/ethnicity of the offender.

Detention on Arrest

It is difficult, on the basis of this analysis, to make definitive statements regarding crime committed and juvenile justice, given the ambiguity inherent in the variable 'seriousness of crime'. A more accurate test of police and judicial discretion involves the decision upon arrest to detain in custody or to release the offender. As mentioned in the methods section, this variable should tap a partly subjective decision by the police and juvenile authorities as to (a) whether the offender is responsible to appear in court on his or her own recognizance, and (b) whether the individual is a danger to society.

Table 6.2 presents the initial model predicting the discretionary decision to detain or release on arrest. It might be expected that such decisions would be made primarily on the basis of seriousness of the crime and an individual's record, and not on the basis of extra-legal concerns. However, race-related decisions to detain on arrest based on the race of the offender, when legal variables are accounted for, should indicate, in part, discriminatory justice.

The variables of interest in a model predicting detention on arrest include the legal concerns of record and seriousness of offence mentioned above, and the extra-legal factors of sex, age, and race. Table 6.2 presents a five-way logit model with race, age, sex, and record. Table 6.3 presents a similar model substituting seriousness of offence for previous conviction. The decision to produce two logit models, isolating record from seriousness of offence, is premised on (a) the necessity of avoiding a table with six variables which would be too complicated to analyse, and (b) the lack of association between record and seriousness of offence at the zero-order level and in a previously run logit model containing race, sex, record, and seriousness of offence. It is also important to note that detention on arrest has been eliminated as a predictor variable from forthcoming analyses. I have run cross-tabulations on the dependent variables with detention on arrest, and I have found no association with plea, adjudication, or disposition. I have, therefore, chosen to eliminate 'detention on arrest' from subsequent causal models. I am confident that the models are not susceptible to specification error.

In Table 6.2, Model 3 is the first model to reveal an accurate correspondence between observed and expected frequencies; this model is responsible for 80% of the baseline chi-square.

The addition of two-way and three-way interactions adds very little to the baseline chi-square and none of these interactions is significant at the .05 level. Model 3, then, is relatively uncomplicated and reveals the strong influence of previous conviction on police decisions to detain; those offenders with previous convictions have a substantially greater than average chance (log odds .907) of being detained on arrest. For Natives, the log odds of being detained (.449) are significantly greater than those for Whites. For Others, the odds (-.448) are less than those for Whites and Natives. These results suggest that the decision to detain on arrest is based primarily on record and race. However, seriousness of offence is an equally plausible basis for police discretion at this level of justice, and Table 6.3 illustrates the model including race, age, sex, and seriousness of offence.

Observation of the chi-square statistic in Table 6.3 reveals that Model 5 which explains 81% of the baseline chi-square is the only model to adequately reproduce the predicted cell means (L^2 .075). As in Model 3, consistent relationships are observed between race and detention: Natives are detained more frequently than are Whites or Others. However, the main effects of race, age, sex, and seriousness of offence are superseded in the two-way interactions with age, sex, and seriousness of offence. As in the analysis of 'arrest for serious crimes' (Table 6.1), the causal influences inherent in these interactions are quite complex, but they are essential to an accurate investigation of discriminatory justice.

The two-way interaction terms between race and non-serious offence suggest that for Natives who commit non-serious crimes, the log odds of being detained on arrest (.565) are significantly greater than for Others and Whites, who both show a less than average chance of being detained, having committed non-serious violations. As well, the interaction between race and sex suggests that males in the Other racial group have a less than average chance of being detained (-.533), when compared to their Native and White counterparts. Overall, sex seems to have little bearing on detention for Natives or Whites, at least at the two-way interaction level.

The final significant two-way interaction, seriousness of offence by sex, shows that males who commit non-serious crimes are detained less often (log odds -.307) than males who commit serious crimes, as would be expected. This term also shows that females who commit serious crimes are detained less often than females who commit non-serious crimes, a somewhat surprising finding. As well, for non-serious offences, females are detained proportionately more than males, while for serious offences males are detained more often than females. This somewhat anomalous treatment of female offenders—females are

Table 6.2 Logit Models of Detention on Arrest by Race, Age, Sex, and Criminal Record (N = 495)

PREDETERMINED VARIABLES	MODEL					
	(1) BASELINE	(2) RACE MAIN EFFECT	(3) ALL MAIN EFFECTS	(4) 2-WAY RACE INTER-ACTION	(5) ALL 2-WAY INTER-ACTION	(6) 3-WAY RACE INTER-ACTION
MAIN EFFECTS						
Constant	.467*	-.444*	-1.043*	-.859*	-.838*	-.810*
Race						
White		-.126	-.001	-.275	-.254	-.227
Native		.407*	.449*	.282	.136	.266
Other		-.281	-.448*	.007	.118	-.039
Age						
12-15			-.143	-.037	.223	.135
Record, Precon						
(Preconviction)			.907*	.829*	.795*	1.020*
Sex						
Male			.222	.046	.035	-.076

Table 6.2 (continued)

	MODEL					
	(1)	(2)	(3)	(4)	(5)	(6)
PREDETERMINED VARIABLES	BASELINE	RACE MAIN EFFECT	ALL MAIN EFFECTS	2-WAY RACE INTER-ACTION	ALL 2-WAY INTER-ACTION	3-WAY RACE INTER-ACTION
INTERACTION EFFECTS						
12-15 by White				−.199	−.223	−.024
12-15 by Native				.098	.082	−.254
12-15 by Other				.101	.141	.278
Precon by White				.162	.139	−.166
Precon by Native				−.173	−.111	−.254
Precon by Other				.011	−.027	.420
Male by White				.214	.199	.285
Male by Native				.312	.420	.439
Male by Other				−.526**	−.619*	−.724
Precon by 12-15					−.185	.110
Precon by Male					.025	−.142
12-15 by Male					−.191	−.330
White, 12-15, Precon						−.435
Native, 12-15, Precon						.005
Other, 12-15, Precon						.430
White, Male, Precon						.270
Native, Male, Precon						−.043
Other, Male, Precon						−.227
White, 12-15, Male						.075
Native, 12-15, Male						.497
Other, 12-15, Male						−.572
L^2	105.50	99.25	20.71	15.99	11.83	4.80
d.f.	23	21	18	12	9	3
prob.	.000	.000	.300	.250	.250	.250
$1-L_i^2/L_j^2$		.059	.804	.848	.888	.955

NOTE: All coefficients are parameters of the additive logit model and are maximum-likelihood estimates calculated using glim (Baker and Nelder 1978). The dichotomous variables are categorized as follows: Detention on Arrest, detained vs released; Age, 12-15 vs 16-18; Record, previous conviction (precon) vs no precon; Sex, male vs female. The variable race is trichotomized into White, Native, and Other.

*Estimate significant at alpha = .05
**Estimate significant at alpha = .10

treated especially harshly for less serious violation—has been documented in previous research (Barnhorst 1980; Geller 1980; Campbell 1981).

On the basis of the two logit models, several extra-legal concerns seem to influence police and court decision to detain on arrest, over and above the obvious legal variables of previous record and seriousness of offence. As seen in Table 6.2, record has an autonomous effect on detention. Table 6.3, as well, shows an influence of seriousness of offence, but this influence appears in combination with extra-legal concerns such as age, sex, and race of the offender. For non-serious offences, Natives appear to be dealt with more harshly than Whites or Others. Also in this category of non-serious offences, males are dealt with less harshly than females, a somewhat surprising finding, which may result from assumptions by judicial officials that non-serious misconduct is normal behaviour for males but abnormal for females and must be dealt with accordingly. This certainly may be reflective of a more paternalistic posture by the courts towards women. For serious offences the opposite is true, with males experiencing the harshest treatment.

Counsel Status

The variable 'counsel status' has important theoretical implications in models predicting judicial outcome. The variable is tested in analyses predicting plea, adjudication, and disposition, the rationale being that private lawyers are more successful than duty counsel in defending their clients. Before we test this proposition, however, it is important to analyse whether all juveniles have equal access to private lawyers, and if disparities in counsel status exist, what factors

Table 6.3 Logit Models of Detention on Arrest by Race, Age, Sex, and Seriousness of Crime (N = 754)

PREDETERMINED VARIABLES	MODEL					
	(1) BASELINE	(2) RACE MAIN EFFECT	(3) ALL MAIN EFFECTS	(4) 2-WAY RACE INTER-ACTION	(5) ALL 2-WAY INTER-ACTION	(6) 3-WAY RACE INTER-ACTION
MAIN EFFECTS						
Constant	-.526*	-.363*	-.828*	-.656*	-.546*	-.418
Race						
White		-.319*	-.349*	-.727*	-.597*	-.814*
Native		.348*	.420*	.548*	.495*	.387
Other		-.029	-.071	.179	.102	.427
Age						
12-15			-.154**	-.067	.146	.238
Offence, Non-Ser						
(Non-Serious)			-.418*	-.408*	-.189	-.275
Sex						
Male			.317*	.083	-.086	-.342

Table 6.3 (continued)

PREDETERMINED VARIABLES	MODEL					
	(1) BASELINE	(2) RACE MAIN EFFECT	(3) ALL MAIN EFFECTS	(4) 2-WAY RACE INTER-ACTION	(5) ALL 2-WAY INTER-ACTION	(6) 3-WAY RACE INTER-ACTION
INTERACTION EFFECTS						
12-15 by White				-.153	-.153	-.031
12-15 by Native				.084	.066	-.286
12-15 by Other				-.069	.087	.317
Non-Ser by White				-.196	-.110	-.167
Non-Ser by Native				.585*	.565*	.797*
Non-Ser by Other				-.389*	-.455*	-.630*
Male by White				.330	.263	.724**
Male by Native				.205	.270	.450
Male by Other				-.535*	-.533*	-1.174*
Non-Ser by 12-15					.137	-.217
Non-Ser by Male					-.307*	-.361**
12-15 by Male					-.157	-.519
White, 12-15, Non-Ser						.612*
Native, 12-15, Non-Ser						-.052
Other, 12-15, Non-Ser						-.560
White, Male, Non-Ser						.350
Native, Male, Non-Ser						-.149
Other, Male, Non-Ser						-.201
White, 12-15, Male						.316
Native, 12-15, Male						.470
Other, 12-15, Male						-.786**
L^2	80.77	68.46	38.30	22.91	15.41	.77
d.f.	23	21	18	12	9	3
prob.	.000	.000	.001	.040	.075	.850
$1-L_i^2/L_j^2$		.152	.526	.716	.809	.990

NOTE: All coefficients are parameters of the additive logit model and are maximum-likelihood estimates calculated using glim (Baker and Nelder 1978). The dichotomous variables are categorized as follows: Detention on Arrest, detained vs released; Age, 12-15 vs 16-18; Seriousness of Offence, non-serious vs serious; Sex, male vs female. The variable race is trichotomized into White, Native, and Other.

*Estimate significant at alpha = .05
**Estimate significant at alpha = .10

determine these disparities. The category of private lawyer/legal aid is referred to as private counsel in the following analysis.

Tables 6.4 and 6.5 present logit models explaining type of legal counsel on the basis of both extra-legal as well as legal variables. The main hypothesis tests the influence of race on access to private lawyers or legal aid (private counsel) versus duty counsel. Included in the analyses, as well, are the legal variables, seriousness of offence and record, and the extra-legal variables: race, age, and sex. To avoid the possibility of zero-cell frequencies in a six-way model, two five-way contingency analyses are used, one with race, record, seriousness of offence, and age (Table 6.4), and the second substituting sex for age (Table 6.5). Initially, a series of four-way logit models was run for the relationship between race and counsel status, using all possible combinations of record, seriousness of offence, sex, and age. In the analyses, I consistently found that age and sex did not significantly interact in the models. This finding, coupled with the absence of zero-order relationship between the two variables (contingency coefficient .027) permits separate tests of these variables. Table 6.4 presents the model testing the main and interaction effects of record, seriousness of offence, age, and race.

Model 4 is the most appropriate model and shows a strong correspondence between actual and predicted cell means (prob. 750). As well, this model accounts for an additional 77% of the baseline chi-square. Here, the interactions between race and previous conviction and between race and age are significant predictors of counsel status, as is the main effect (−.430) of seriousness of offence. The effect of seriousness of offence suggests that for those juveniles who have committed non-serious crimes, the chances of retaining private counsel are significantly lower than for juveniles committing serious offences, as would be expected. The interaction between previous conviction and the Other race category reveals that repeat-offenders in the Other racial group have substantially greater access to private counsel (log odds .655) than do Natives or Whites. The interactions between race and age suggest that for young White and young Native offenders, the likelihood (.515 and .493 respectively) of retaining private counsel are significantly greater than average, the opposite being true for young offenders in the Other race category. However in the sixteen- to eighteen-year-old age group, the Other race category has a substantially greater access (log odds 1.008) to private counsel than do Natives or Whites.

Table 6.5 shows the logit model replicating the previous analysis with the exception that sex is substituted for age.

Model 5 is the first model to show an accurate fit of expected and actual cell means; this model accounts for 80% of the baseline chi-square. In Model 5, the main effect of seriousness of offence is shown to be conditioned by sex. For male offenders who have committed non-serious violations, the odds of accessing private counsel are less (−.397) than those for females committing non-serious crimes. As well, for males committing serious violations, access to private counsel is greater than for females committing serious offences. Sex also acts in association with previous conviction, which indicates that males with previous convictions are more likely than average to have private counsel while their female counterparts are less likely (.269). As a corollary, for first-offenders, males are less likely than females to have private counsel. In this model as well, an interaction between non-serious offence and the racial category of Other is significant, an effect which was not significant in the previous logit model, Table 6.4. In Table 6.5, for those in the Other racial group who commit non-serious crimes, the likelihood of retaining private counsel is significantly less (−.413) than for Natives or Whites. Similarly, for those in the Other racial group who commit serious crimes, the chances of having private counsel are greater than for Natives or Whites. The greater access to private counsel that the Other racial group has in both models is qualified somewhat by the type of crime committed, and indicates, along with other findings in these two tables, that access to private lawyers is not uniform across gender and racial groups. Quite clearly, we find here that the access to private counsel is based on social as well as legal factors. The next step in analysing counsel status is to see whether private lawyers are more effective in intervening for their clients than are court-appointed lawyers.

Plea

Tables 6.6 and 6.7 contain logit analyses predicting 'plea', guilty or innocent. As explained in the methodology section, two analyses are presented, isolating the effects of seriousness of crime from criminal record. Table 6.6 shows the model containing race, presence of parent, counsel status, and seriousness of offence.

Table 6.4 Logit Models of Private Counsel by Race, Age, Previous Conviction, and Seriousness of Offence (N = 486)

	MODEL					
	(1)	(2)	(3)	(4)	(5)	(6)
PREDETERMINED		RACE	ALL	2-WAY RACE	ALL 2-WAY	3-WAY RACE
VARIABLES	BASELINE	MAIN EFFECT	MAIN EFFECTS	INTER-ACTION	INTER-ACTION	INTER-ACTION
MAIN EFFECTS						
Constant	−.057	−.033	−.197	−.390*	−.471*	−.701
Race						
White		−.085	−.102	.177	.227	.493
Native		−.290**	−.266	−.090	−.143	−.325
Other		.375*	.368*	−.087	−.084	−.168
Record, Precon						
(Preconviction)			.183*	.502*	.635*	.787**
Offence, Non-Ser						
(Non-Serious)			−.305*	−.430*	−.520*	−.728**
Age						
12-15			−.147	−.567*	−.583*	−.871**

Table 6.4 (continued)

PREDETERMINED VARIABLES	(1) BASELINE	(2) RACE MAIN EFFECT	(3) ALL MAIN EFFECTS	(4) 2-WAY RACE INTER-ACTION	(5) ALL 2-WAY INTER-ACTION	(6) 3-WAY RACE INTER-ACTION
MODEL						
INTERACTION EFFECTS						
Precon by White				-.360	-.358	-.537
Precon by Native				-.295	-.280	-.017
Precon by Other				.655*	.638*	.554
Non-Ser by White				.225	.274	.522
Non-Ser by Native				.128	.070	-.152
Non-Ser by Other				-.353	-.344	-.370
12-15 by White				.515*	.517*	.866**
12-15 by Native				.493*	.500*	.649
12-15 by Other				-1.008*	-1.017*	-1.515*
Precon by Non-Ser					.193	.343
Non-Ser by 12-15					-.014	-.351
Precon by 12-15					.050	.125
White, Precon, Non-Ser						-.163
Native, Pre-con, Non-Ser						.345
Other, Precon, Non-Ser						-.182
White, Non-Ser, 12-15						.431
Native, Non-Ser, 12-15						.341
Other, Non-Ser, 12-15						-.772**
White, Precon, 12-15						-.152
Native, Precon, 12-15						.222
Other, Precon, 12-15						-.070
L^2	38.40	35.26	23.07	8.85	6.58	.52
d.f.	23	21	18	12	9	3
prob.	.025	.025	.150	.750	.650	.900
$1-L_i^2/L_j^2$		.082	.602	.770	.829	.986

NOTE: All coefficients are parameters of the additive logit model and are maximum-likelihood estimates calculated using glim (Baker and Nelder 1978). The dichotomous variables are categorized as follows: Counsel Status, Private vs Duty Counsel/Other; Age, 12-15 vs 16-18; Record, previous conviction (Precon) vs no previous conviction; Seriousness of Offence, non-serious vs serious. The variable race is trichotomized into White, Native, and Other.

*Estimate significant at alpha = .05
**Estimate significant at alpha = .10

The preferred model, Model 4, accurately duplicates the predicted cell means and explains an additional 17% of the baseline chi-square over and above the main effects model (.649 to .821). This percentage increase is accounted for by the significant effects of Native-parent and Other-parent (-.948 and .703

respectively). These coefficients indicate that race has an effect on plea, and that this effect is in combination with presence of parent. For Native offenders whose parents are present in court, the likelihood of pleading guilty is substantially lower (–.948) than for Natives whose parents are not present. For the Other racial group, the relationship is reversed, with the presence of a parent increasing the likelihood of a guilty plea. The two other significant coefficients in this model are for record (–.315) and counsel status (–.780). The latter coefficient suggests that the decision to plead not guilty is more probable given access to private counsel. It is possible that the decision to plead not guilty is enhanced by the chances of success that private or legal aid lawyers promise. Equally plausible is the possibility that the decision to plead not guilty encourages the procurement of private counsel or legal aid versus the assignment of duty counsel. The main effect of record suggests that previous contact with the legal system (and the likelihood of greater familiarity with the system as a result) encourages offenders to plead not guilty (–.315). This coefficient, however, is significant only at the .10 level and significant only for this model.

Table 6.7 further tests the prediction of plea by introducing seriousness of offence into the model.

For this logit model, Model 3 explains 78% of the baseline chi-square. Model 4 contributes only an additional 6% to the baseline chi-square over the main effects model, Model 3. However, the chi-square probability of .925 illustrates a

Table 6.5 Logit Models of Private Counsel by Race, Sex, Previous Conviction, and Seriousness of Offence (N = 676)

PREDETERMINED VARIABLES	MODEL					
	(1) BASELINE	(2) RACE MAIN EFFECT	(3) ALL MAIN EFFECTS	(4) 2-WAY RACE INTER-ACTION	(5) ALL 2-WAY INTER-ACTION	(6) 3-WAY RACE INTER-ACTION
MAIN EFFECTS						
Constant	–.006	.183	–.234	–.152	–.088	–.120
Race						
White		–.175	–.171	–.277	–.200	–.195
Native		–.272**	–.266**	–.309	–.304	–.211
Other		.447*	.437*	.586*	.504*	.406
Record, Precon						
(Preconviction)			.147**	.198	–.004	.167
Offence, Non-Ser						
Non-Serious			–.261*	–.422*	–.136	–.223
Sex						
Male			.253*	.005	–.144	–.092

Table 6.5 (continued)

PREDETERMINED VARIABLES	MODEL					
	(1) BASELINE	(2) RACE MAIN EFFECT	(3) ALL MAIN EFFECTS	(4) 2-WAY RACE INTER-ACTION	(5) ALL 2-WAY INTER-ACTION	(6) 3-WAY RACE INTER-ACTION
INTERACTION EFFECTS						
Precon by White				−.079	−.065	−.278
Precon by Native				−.025	.019	−.126
Precon by Other				.104	.046	.404
Non-Ser by White				.177	.185	.261
Non-Ser by Native				.255	.228	.339
Non-Ser by Other				−.432*	−.413*	−.600**
Male by White				.305	.234	.201
Male by Native				.244	.200	.179
Male by Other				−.549*	−.434**	−.380
Precon by Non-Ser					.032	−.068
Precon by Male					.269*	−.033
Non-Ser by Male					−.397*	−.318
White, Precon, Non-Ser						.139
Native, Precon, Non-Ser						−.029
Other, Precon, Non-Ser						−.110
White, Non-Ser, Male						−.067
Native, Non-Ser, Male						−.018
Other, Non-Ser, Male						.085
White, Precon, Male						.394
Native, Precon, Male						.135
Other, Precon, Male						−.529
L^2	48.96	43.60	26.22	21.28	10.03	6.83
d.f.	23	21	18	12	9	3
prob.	.000	.005	.075	.050	.300	.075
$1-L_i^2/L_j^2$		.109	.464	.565	.795	.860

NOTE: All coefficients are parameters of the additive logit model and are maximum-likelihood estimates calculated using glim (Baker and Nelder 1978). The dichotomous variables are categorized as follows: Counsel Status, private vs duty counsel/other; Sex, male vs female; Record, previous conviction (Precon) vs no previous conviction; Seriousness of Offence, non-serious vs serious. The variable race is trichotomized into White, Native, and Other.

*Estimate significant at alpha = .05
**Estimate significant at alpha = .10

highly accurate fit between predicted and observed cell means. As well, the interaction between parent and Native is significant at the .05 level. This coefficient corroborates the significant interaction effect found in Table 6.6 for Natives with parents present in court, and indicates once again that the presence

Table 6.6 Logit Models of Plea of Guilty by Race, Presence of Parent, Previous Conviction, and Private Counsel (N = 468)

PREDETERMINED VARIABLES	MODEL					
	(1) BASELINE	(2) RACE MAIN EFFECT	(3) ALL MAIN EFFECTS	(4) RACE/ PARENT INTER-ACTION	(5) 2-WAY RACE INTER-ACTION	(6) ALL 2-WAY INTER-ACTION
MAIN EFFECTS						
Constant	2.050*	2.013*	2.373*	2.513*	2.634*	2.648*
Race						
White		.053	−.062	−.212	−.327	−.310
Native		.034	.061	.433	.167	−.042
Other		−.087	.001	−.221	.160	.352
Family Presence						
Parent			.288**	.181	.218	.510
Record, Precon						
(Preconviction)			−.284	−.315**	−.147	−.061
Counsel Status						
Private			−.790*	−.780*	−1.076*	−1.067*
INTERACTION EFFECTS						
Parent by White				.245	.198	.137
Parent by Native				−.948*	−.887*	−.894*
Parent by Other				.703*	.689**	.757**
Precon by White					−.290	−.394
Precon by Native					.314	.411
Precon by Other					−.024	−.017
Private by White					.384	.374
Private by Native					.041	.219
Private by Other					−.425	−.593
Parent by Private						−.286
Parent by Precon						−.156
Private by Precon						−.070
L^2	47.60	47.52	16.71	8.52	5.83	2.88
d.f.	23	21	18	16	12	9
prob.	.005	.001	.600	.925	.925	.960
$1-L_i^2/L_j^2$		.002	.649	.821	.876	.939

NOTE: All coefficients are parameters of the additive logit model and are maximum-likelihood estimates calculated using glim (Baker and Nelder 1978). The dichotomous variables are categorized as follows: Family Presence, parent vs none; Record, previous conviction (precon) vs no previous conviction; Counsel Status, private vs duty counsel. The variable race is trichotomized into White, Native, and Other.

*Estimate significant at alpha = .05
**Estimate significant at alpha = .10

of a parent has a substantial impact on Native offenders' decisions to plead not guilty. Such is not the case for White or Other offenders. As well, for Models 3 and 4 the strong isolated influence of counsel status (−.947) is again evident, with private lawyers most likely to determine not-guilty pleas. Surprisingly, seriousness of offence is not significantly related to plea; this finding is consistent across models for both main and interaction effects.

In conclusion, it appears that the decision to plead either guilty or not guilty is explained by several factors: (a) access to private counsel as compared to duty counsel, with the suggestion that private lawyers or legal aid lawyers are more likely to foster pleas of not guilty; (b) the presence of a family member (for Natives only) because the presence of a parent is more likely to encourage a plea of not guilty; and (c) previous conviction, which appears to have a small effect on plea, although this effect is less substantial and less significant than expected.

Adjudication

Table 6.8 presents the logit model predicting conviction versus withdrawal of charges. This model is based on all young offenders in the analysis who have pleaded guilty.

Both Models 3 and 6 fail to achieve significance at the .10 level, illustrating in

Table 6.7 Logit Models of Plea of Guilty by Race, Presence of Parent, Seriousness of Offence, and Private Counsel (N = 581)

	MODEL					
	(1)	(2)	(3)	(4)	(5)	(6)
PREDETERMINED VARIABLES	BASELINE	RACE MAIN EFFECT	ALL MAIN EFFECTS	2-WAY RACE INTER-ACTION	ALL 2-WAY INTER-ACTION	3-WAY RACE INTER-ACTION
MAIN EFFECTS						
Constant	1.162*	1.215*	1.479*	1.753*	1.776*	2.307*
Race						
White		−.103	−.164	−.486**	−.473**	−.996*
Native		.228	.251	.656**	.638**	.835
Other		−.125	−.087	−.170	−.165	.161
Family Presence						
Parent			.254*	.165	.157	−.563
Offence, Non-Ser						
(Non-Serious)			.007	.215	.165	.470
Counsel Status						
Private			−.886*	−.947*	−.853*	−1.466*

Table 6.7 (continued)

	MODEL					
	(1)	(2)	(3)	(4)	(5)	(6)
PREDETERMINED VARIABLES	BASELINE	RACE MAIN EFFECT	ALL MAIN EFFECTS	2-WAY RACE INTER-ACTION	ALL 2-WAY INTER-ACTION	3-WAY RACE INTER-ACTION
INTERACTION EFFECTS						
Parent by White				.158	.159	.927**
Parent by Native				-.422*	-.405*	-.119
Parent by Other				.264	.246	-.808
Non-Ser by White				-.247	-.240	-.549
Non-Ser by Native				-.101	-.134	-.520
Non-Ser by Other				.348	.374	1.069
Private by White				.087	.059	.672
Private by Native				-.496	-.502	-.070
Private by Other				.409	.443	.602
Parent by Private					-.106	.040
Parent by Non-Ser					-.116	-.844
Private by Non-Ser					.198	-.157
White, Parent, Non-Ser						.774
Native, Parent, Non-Ser						.100
Other, Parent, Non-Ser						-.874
White, Private, Non-Ser						.356
Native, Private, Non-Ser						1.068
Other, Private, Non-Ser						-1.424**
White, Parent, Private						-.206
Native, Parent, Private						-.234
Other, Parent, Private						.440
L^2	106.70	104.90	23.55	15.32	11.68	1.71
d.f.	23	21	18	12	9	3
prob.	.000	.000	.150	.925	.950	.985
$1-L_i^2/L_j^2$		.017	.779	.856	.891	.984

NOTE: All coefficients are parameters of the additive logit model and are maximum-likelihood estimates calculated using glim (Baker and Nelder 1978). The dichotomous variables are categorized as follows: Family Presence, parent vs none; Seriousness of Offence, non-ser vs serious; Counsel Status, private vs duty counsel. The variable race is trichotomized into White, Native, and Other.

*Estimate significant at alpha = .05
**Estimate significant at alpha = .10

both cases a high correspondence between actual and predicted cell means. Model 3, however, accounts for only 37% of the baseline chi-square whereas Model 6 explains 89%. Also, for Model 6, several two-way interaction terms are significant, a finding substantively important because it illustrates that the

Table 6.8 Logit Models of Conviction by Race, Seriousness of Offence, and Private Counsel (N = 543)

VARIABLES	MODEL					
	(1) BASELINE	(2) RACE MAIN EFFECT	(3) ALL MAIN EFFECTS	(4) RACE/SER INTER-ACTION	(5) 2-WAY RACE INTER-ACTION	(6) ALL 2-WAY INTER-ACTION
MAIN EFFECTS						
Constant	2.331*	2.197*	2.251*	2.248*	2.589*	2.811*
Race						
White		.269	.232	.213	-.119	-.188
Native		-.227	-.261	-.174	-.521	-.526
Other		-.042	.029	-.039	.640	.714
Offence, Non-Ser						
(Non-Serious)			-.040	-.031	-.146	-.229
Counsel Status						
Private			-.333*	-.334*	-.766	-.735
INTERACTION EFFECTS						
Non-Ser by White				-.066	.036	.101
Non-Ser by Native				.191	.389	.659**
Non-Ser by Other				-.125	-.425	-.760*
Private by White					.377	.452
Private by Native					.791	1.029**
Private by Other					-1.168*	-1.481*
Non-Ser by Private						.438*
L^2	17.38	15.45	11.02	10.57	6.83	1.93
d.f.	11	9	7	5	3	2
prob.	.075	.075	.150	.075	.075	.400
$1-L_i^2/L_j^2$		.111	.366	.392	.607	.889

NOTE: All coefficients are parameters of the additive logit model and are maximum-likelihood estimates calculated using glim (Baker and Nelder 1978). The dichotomous variables are categorized as follows: Adjudication, convicted vs charge withdrawn; Counsel Status, private vs duty counsel; Seriousness of Offence, serious vs non-serious. The ethnicity variable is trichotomized into White, Native, and Other.

*Estimate significant at alpha = .05
**Estimate significant at alpha = .10

main effects of legal variables such as seriousness of offence are often qualified by interaction with race. The first interaction term between seriousness of offence and race category indicates that Native offenders who have committed non-serious violations are more likely to be convicted (.659) than Whites or Others. As well, in the non-serious offence category, Other offenders have a substantially greater chance of having charges withdrawn than do Natives or Whites. This finding is consistent with recent research that suggests that Native youths and adults are more likely than non-Native youths and adults to be arrested and convicted for minor violations (Yerbury and Griffiths 1991). Amongst those offenders committing serious crimes, members of the Other category stand a greater than average chance of being convicted. For serious crimes, Natives have a greater than average chance of being acquitted.

As has been hypothesized, the presence of private counsel appears to have a deterrent effect on conviction, an effect that interacts with race and seriousness of offence. For Native juvenile offenders with private counsel, the log odds of being convicted are greater than for Whites or Others. Private counsel appears to be most advantageous for members of the Other racial group, whose chances of acquittal are greatly enhanced by private counsel as compared to duty counsel. By the same token, duty counsel is least advantageous for Others and most advantageous for Natives.

A related finding in this analysis of race and conviction is that seriousness of offence and counsel status jointly influence legal outcome. Private lawyers or legal aid lawyers enhance the chances of acquittal for those committing serious crimes. For those committing non-serious crimes, however, the chances of being acquitted (.438) are greater with duty counsel than with private lawyers. It would appear that private counsel produces advantage mostly for those committing serious crimes.

In conclusion, conviction or acquittal is based, at least to some degree, on type of counsel, race, and seriousness of offence. Private legal counsel or legal aid appears to be most advantageous for the Other racial group and least advantageous for Natives. Also, for those committing serious crimes, such counsel appears to be much more effective in determining acquittal than does court-appointed duty counsel. Natives who commit non-serious crimes and who have access to private counsel or legal aid are relatively disadvantaged. Advantage, in the context of adjudication, appears mostly for Others, especially for those committing non-serious crimes and for those having access to private lawyers or legal aid.

Disposition

Tables 6.9 and 6.10 describe the logit models predicting unconditional release. Table 6.9 presents the main and interaction effects of race, previous conviction, presence of parent and counsel status.

Model 5 is the preferred model here and although it departs from significance only marginally (.085), it does account for 77.6% of the baseline chi-square. The effects in this model are relatively simple. The main effect of race observed in the first four models is apparent in Model 5 as well. Being Native has a consistently significant influence on release; the negative coefficients suggests that for Natives, the likelihood of unqualified release is less than for Whites or Others. The finding suggests that Natives are most susceptible to dispositions that involve incarceration or probationary scrutiny. Model 5 illustrates, however, that the influence of race on disposition occurs in interaction with family presence. The odds of unqualified release are greater for Natives with parents present (.596) than for Natives who appear alone in court. Similarly, Whites or Others who appear alone have a greater chance of release without scrutiny than do Natives. In Table 6.10 the interaction term reappears and is consistently significant. Lastly, in this model, we observe the isolated influence of record which suggests that if the young offender has had a previous conviction, the likelihood of unconditional release is substantially lower than for a first offence, a not unexpected finding.

Table 6.10 presents a series of logit models similar to those presented in Table 6.9 with the exception that record is replaced by seriousness of offence.

Here, as in Table 6.9, the main effect of being Native appears consistently across models, indicating again that cases involving Native juveniles are disposed of relatively harshly. Model 4 is the preferred model and is characterized by a series of interaction effects between race, seriousness of offence, and family presence.

As mentioned previously, the main effect of being Native remains significant for this preferred model. As well, the main effects of parental presence and seriousness of offence are statistically significant, the former suggesting that the presence of a parent or guardian in court increases the chances of unconditional

Table 6.9 Logit Models of Unconditional Release by Race, Presence of Parent, Previous Conviction, and Private Counsel (N = 365)

	MODEL					
	(1)	(2)	(3)	(4)	(5)	(6)
PREDETERMINED VARIABLES	BASELINE	RACE MAIN EFFECT	ALL MAIN EFFECTS	2-WAY RACE INTER-ACTION	ALL 2-WAY INTER-ACTION	3-WAY RACE INTER-ACTION
MAIN EFFECTS						
Constant	.291*	.073	.308	.325	.355	.440
Race						
White		.418*	.266	.286	.325	.234
Native		−.466*	−.429**	−.640*	−.661*	−.429
Other		.048	.163	.354	.336	.195
Family Presence						
Parent			.013	.098	.043	.123
Record, Precon						
(Preconviction)			−.700*	−.803*	−.864*	−1.197*
Counsel Status						
Private			−.217**	−.167	−.243	−.629

Table 6.9 (continued)

	MODEL					
	(1)	(2)	(3)	(4)	(5)	(6)
PREDETERMINED VARIABLES	BASELINE	RACE MAIN EFFECT	ALL MAIN EFFECTS	2-WAY RACE INTER-ACTION	ALL 2-WAY INTER-ACTION	3-WAY RACE INTER-ACTION
INTERACTION EFFECTS						
Parent by White				−.212	−.219	−.244
Parent by Native				.565**	.596**	.783
Parent by Other				−.353	−.377	−.539
Precon by White				.182	.173	.552
Precon by Native				−.100	−.116	−.184
Precon by Other				−.082	−.057	−.368
Private by White				−.091	−.084	.370
Private by Native				−.003	.008	−.760
Private by Other				.094	.076	.390
Parent by Private					.177	.305
Parent by Precon					.122	.329
Private by Precon					−.082	.295
White, Parent, Precon						−.300
Native, Parent, Precon						−.467
Other, Parent, Precon						.767**
White, Private, Precon						−.585
Native, Private, Precon						1.366*
Other, Private, Precon						−.781
White, Parent, Private						−.181
Native, Parent, Private						.024
Other, Parent, Private						.157
L^2	83.98	73.45	29.05	22.08	18.83	.097
d.f.	23	21	18	12	9	3
prob.	.000	.000	.025	.025	.085	.999
$1-L_i^2/L_j^2$		.125	.654	.737	.776	.988

NOTE: All coefficients are parameters of the additive logit model and are maximum-likelihood estimates calculated using glim (Baker and Nelder 1978). The dichotomous variables are categorized as follows: Adjudication, unconditional release vs incarceration or release under scrutiny; Record, previous conviction vs no previous conviction; Family Presence, parent vs none; Counsel Status, private vs duty counsel. The variable race is trichotomized into White, Native, and Other.

 *Estimate significant at alpha = .05
**Estimate significant at alpha = .10

release, and the latter suggesting that the probability of release is greatest for those committing non-serious crimes, once again not unexpected findings. Model 4, however, shows these main effects to be qualified by their interaction with one another.

For example, the interaction terms between parent and race suggest that for Natives with parents present, the odds of being released (.434) are greater than for Others and significantly greater than for Whites (−.544). As well, for Native offenders who appear without a parent or guardian, the probability of being incarcerated or released with scrutiny is substantially greater than for Whites or Others. The presence of a parent appears to have no effect for the Other racial group. However, for those youth committing non-serious crimes, members of the Other racial group are most likely to be released unconditionally (.461), while for Whites, the opposite is true. On the contrary, white offenders who commit serious offences have the greatest advantage in that the odds of their release are better than for Natives or Others. Interestingly, counsel status does not have a significant effect throughout this analysis, either in main or interaction effect.

In general, these two logit models reveal some interesting findings regarding disposition. First, Natives appear to experience consistently more severe dispositions than Whites or Others despite legal and court-specific influences. As well, Native juveniles receive more severe dispositions when unaccompanied by a parent, as compared to Whites or Others. Simply put, Native juveniles benefit the most from the presence of a family member or guardian. Secondly, cases are disposed of partly on the basis of seriousness of offence and partly on the basis of record. As would be expected, a previous conviction decreases the

Table 6.10 Logit Models of Unconditional Release by Race, Presence of Parent, Seriousness of Offence, and Private Counsel (N = 440)

PREDETERMINED VARIABLES	MODEL					
	(1) BASELINE	(2) RACE MAIN EFFECT	(3) ALL MAIN EFFECTS	(4) 2-WAY RACE INTER-ACTION	(5) ALL 2-WAY INTER-ACTION	(6) 3-WAY RACE INTER-ACTION
MAIN EFFECTS						
Constant	.386*	.133	.276**	.352**	.294	.225
Race						
White		.430*	.385*	.307	.366	.419
Native		−.295	−.372**	−.584*	−.591*	−.493
Other		−.135	−.013	.277	.225	.074
Family Presence						
Parent			.100	.319**	.226	.012
Offence, Non-Ser						
(Non-Serious)			.353*	.745*	.790*	.905**
Counsel Status						
Private			−.271*	−.065	−.107	−.097

Table 6.10 (continued)

	MODEL					
	(1)	(2)	(3)	(4)	(5)	(6)
PREDETERMINED VARIABLES	BASELINE	RACE MAIN EFFECT	ALL MAIN EFFECTS	2-WAY RACE INTER-ACTION	ALL 2-WAY INTER-ACTION	3-WAY RACE INTER-ACTION
INTERACTION EFFECTS						
Parent by White				−.393*	−.400*	−.151
Parent by Native				.434**	.510*	.707**
Parent by Other				−.041	−.110	−.556
Non-Ser by White				−.544*	−.505*	−.663
Non-Ser by Native				−.014	.044	.158
Non-Ser by Other				.558*	.461**	.505
Private by White				−.278	−.258	−.314
Private by Native				−.087	−.059	.095
Private by Other				.365	.317	.219
Parent by Private					.023	−.242
Parent by Non-Ser					−.269*	−.783*
Private by Non-Ser					−.049	−.146
White, Parent, Non-Ser						.604
Native, Parent, Non-Ser						.206
Other, Parent, Non-Ser						−.810**
White, Private, Non-Ser						.037
Native, Private, Non-Ser						.390
Other, Private, Non-Ser						−.427
White, Parent, Private						.299
Native, Parent, Private						.181
Other, Parent, Private						−.480
L^2	56.42	47.02	26.09	13.23	8.30	3.43
d.f.	23	21	18	12	9	3
prob.	.000	.000	.075	.35	.25	.60
$1-L_i^2/L_j^2$		.167	.538	.766	.853	.939

NOTE: All coefficients are parameters of the additive logit model and are maximum-likelihood estimates calculated using glim (Baker and Nelder 1978). The dichotomous variables are categorized as follows: Adjudication, unconditional release vs incarceration or release under scrutiny; Family Presence, parent vs none; Seriousness of Offence, non-ser vs serious; Counsel Status, private vs duty counsel. The variable race is trichotomized into White, Native, and Other.

*Estimate significant at alpha = .05
**Estimate significant at alpha = .10

probability of unconditional release as does the commission of a more serious offence. For Natives who have been assigned duty counsel, a criminal record renders them especially disadvantaged when compared to Whites or Others in the same category. Furthermore, the commission of a serious offence negatively affects the chances of release for the Other racial group as compared to Natives or Whites.

Finally, it is interesting to note that counsel status shows no significant main or two-way interaction effects in either preferred model in 6.9 or 6.10. I would have expected that intervention by private lawyers or legal aid would have a greater impact on disposition, similar to the influence that counsel status was found to have on adjudication. However, this does not appear to be the case.

Summary

Seriousness of Crime

(1) From the youth court data, the position that male youth commit more serious crimes than females (crimes known to the police) holds true only for repeat-offenders. Amongst first-offenders, females commit and are arrested for more serious crimes than are males.

(2) Amongst offenders between the ages of twelve and fifteen, Whites commit and are arrested for more serious crimes than are Natives or Others. As well, Others in this age category stand a substantially less than average chance of being arrested for serious crime. For the older age category, Whites have the least chance of being arrested for serious crime, while Others have the greatest chance.

(3) On first offence, Natives have a greater than average chance of being arrested for a serious crime, while Others are the most immune to arrest for such crimes. For the category of repeat-offenders, Natives are less likely to commit and be arrested for serious offences than are non-Natives.

Detention on Arrest

(1) As would be expected, criminal record has an independent effect on detention, with repeat-offenders being detained more often than first-offenders.

(2) In general, Natives are detained more often than average, and the Other category of youth are detained less often. This phenomenon is especially apparent for the non-serious crime category.

(3) For non-serious offences, males are detained less often than females, the corollary being true for serious offences.

(4) Males in the Other racial category stand a less than average chance of detainment on arrest compared to Natives or Whites.

Counsel Status

(1) Access to private lawyers or legal aid is greater for youth who commit serious crimes and for youth who have previous convictions. This association depends

on the sex of the offender; the relationship holds true only for males. For females, the opposite is true, with serious crime and previous conviction reducing the offender's chances of retaining private counsel or legal aid.

(2) The Other racial group has greater access to private lawyers or legal aid for cases involving serious crime and for cases in which the offender has a previous conviction. Otherwise, this group, when characterized by non-serious violation and first offence, has a less than average chance of retaining a private lawyer.

(3) The direct influence of race on counsel status is somewhat dependent on age. For the twelve to fifteen age range, Whites and Natives have the greatest chance of retaining private counsel. For the older group, Others have a substantially greater likelihood of accessing private counsel or legal aid.

Plea

(1) Youth with previous records are less likely to plead guilty than are first offenders.

(2) Young offenders with private counsel or legal aid are less likely to plead guilty than are those assigned duty counsel.

(3) When parents are present at judicial proceedings, Native offenders are less likely to plead guilty than are Whites or Others. As a corollary, Native offenders who appear in court without parental support are more likely than average to plead guilty when compared with Whites or Others.

Adjudication

(1) Private lawyers or legal aid lawyers are most beneficial for those committing serious crimes.

(2) Of those youth who commit non-serious crime, Natives have a greater likelihood of being convicted than do Whites or Others. As well, in this non-serious category, Others have a much lower chance of conviction than average.

(3) Private lawyers or legal aid appear to be most beneficial for members of the Other racial group, and least beneficial for Natives, in procuring withdrawal of charges.

Disposition

(1) Native offenders are consistently more susceptible to dispositions involving incarceration or continued scrutiny. (2) For Native offenders, the probability of unqualified release is enhanced by the presence of a parent or guardian much more than for Whites or Others.

(3) Of those youth who commit non-serious crimes, the Other group stands the greatest chance of unconditional release, while Whites have the lowest chance of such a disposition.

Conclusions

In general, this study reveals the influence of extra-legal variables in judicial outcomes. Biases generally appear against Natives and, for the most part, in favour of those in the non-White, non-Native category. The suggestion that these biases are explained by higher crime rates and more serious types of crimes committed by Natives (Boldt *et al.* 1983) is not revealed in this research. On the contrary, as repeat-offenders, Natives commit less serious crimes than non-Natives, but they are dealt with more harshly when such crimes are committed.

My research reveals that the importance of socio-economic power is manifested at the policing level, and is to some degree, at least, based on the race of the accused. It would appear that in confrontations with the police, Native juveniles are assumed by the police to be relatively powerless and, consequently, able to be processed with less difficulty than are other racial groups (Chambliss 1969). My results suggest that Native youth, relative to their non-Native counterparts, are selected for harsher scrutiny by the police, especially those youth who commit non-serious violations. It is worth reiterating that, in the context of disparities in treatment, non-serious violations have been shown to be relatively typical of all youth cultures despite race, class and gender, and that some police decisions are based on considerations other than crime commission. A major premise of the labelling theory approach to criminogenesis is that social control agencies like the police, through the processes of selective detection and publication, not only produce given rates of crime, but also contribute to the psychological process whereby vulnerable individuals come to internalize society's negative labels. Although my data do not test labelling theory, I argue that certain categories of individuals, like Native youths, are isolated more often than others for public scrutiny.

Legal privilege also occurs on the basis of family status. The presence of a family member or guardian in court appears to have a substantial impact on judicial outcomes. Hackler and Paranjape (1984) have suggested that judicial reactions to race are simply reactions to judgements about family situations. My results support this contention. The presence of a family member is most beneficial for Native youth, a finding that suggests that it is especially incumbent on Native youth to prove their family stability. For Whites or Others, family stability is much more often presumed. This contention is also supported by the evidence that Natives committing non-serious violations are detained more often than Whites or Others. It is plausible that judicial officials make assumptions that Native families are either absent or nonsupportive to the extent that such families will not endeavour to have the offender return for adjudication. These findings support the work of LaPrairie (1983) and Cruikshank (1981) that judicial officials make assumptions about Native family situations, and that such assumptions partly determine judicial decisions. The findings regarding parental presence in court also support the position that the presence of a guardian seems to suggest a more powerful, more united front to the court system.

Power also appears to translate into privilege through access to committed and competent legal counsel; avoidance of prosecution is more a matter of legal competency (determined by both time and dedication) and less that of guilt or innocence. Previous research has suggested that preferential treatment on the basis of extra-legal variables such as social class is in part fostered by the adversarial system, because access to private lawyers affords individuals advantage over access to duty counsel (Dootjes, Erickson, and Fox 1972; Erickson 1975). My research would support this position, especially with respect to race. Access to counsel is determined partly by the race of the accused, with non-Native, non-White youth having the greatest access to private lawyers or legal aid and Native youth the least. As a result, I contend that Native youth, when confronted by the judiciary, have less access to committed and competent counsel than do non-Native youth, and the former are more likely to experience severe treatment. Furthermore, this research has revealed how the influence of counsel status is manifested; offenders with private counsel or legal aid are less likely to plead guilty and less likely to receive severe dispositions. In summary, private counsel is expensive, and accessing both private counsel and legal aid involves some knowledge of and sophistication within the system. Individuals who are unfamiliar with the legal system, who are not exposed to help and advice, and who cannot afford to retain private counsel are at a disadvantage; cultural and racial difference and low socio-economic standing foster that disadvantage.

Previous research has argued that despite counsel status, lack of sophistication with legal procedures places certain juveniles at a disadvantage in a rather complex judicial system (Langley, Thomas, and Parkinson 1978). The results in my study regarding plea suggest, quite strongly, that individuals who have previously been exposed to the legal system are much more likely to enter a plea of not guilty, and consequently assume an offensive posture in defending themselves. First-offenders are the least likely to understand the vagaries of the system, and consequently they are less willing to defend themselves, especially those offenders who are unable to afford private counsel or who do not have the knowledge and support to access legal aid.

A common concern throughout this research has been the influence that extra-legal variables have on judicial outcomes for youth committing non-serious violations. Race appears to have a consistent influence on decisions at various stages of the judicial process. Natives apprehended in the non-serious category of crime are detained on arrest at a greater rate, are more likely to be convicted, and are more likely to receive severe dispositions than are non-Natives. It is important to elaborate on this discussion of race by analysing the nature of justice as it is applied to those youth who are neither Native nor White. The Other racial group seems to fare relatively well in the system, having greater access to private counsel or legal aid, suffering less detention on arrest, and receiving less severe dispositions than Natives or Whites.

Although this research has concentrated on race as the major extra-legal variable, the results suggest that pre-judgements are also based somewhat on the sex and age of the offender, although the influence of age is slight. The results in my study regarding sex, however, suggest that females are dealt with more harshly than males, possibly reflecting the paternalistic nature of youth courts and the nature of jurisprudence in general.

It is apparent from this research that youth courts apply the law with discretion and prejudice. Chambliss (1969) and Turk (1969) have suggested that the crime control system victimizes those who can be processed with the least difficulty, namely youth who are assumed to have low socio-economic and political power and who are unfamiliar with a complex legal system, or at least who are perceived to be disaffiliated from individuals who can offer aid and support. My findings endorse their position. At one point or another, the offender's race, social class, age, and sex, influence judicial outcomes. Despite the fact that the Young Offenders Act was implemented to ensure equal treatment under the law, it is apparent that extra-legal factors have a substantial impact on judicial decisions, targeting certain categories of youth for especially harsh treatment. Although I have not tested labelling theory in this book, I maintain that legal scrutiny may exacerbate criminal conduct. Recognition of the phenomenon of discriminatory justice may help explain some of the disparities in crime statistics in Canada based on race. Although I am fully aware of the impact that structural disadvantage has on actual street crime commission, I maintain that, on the basis of the research findings presented here, a renewed interest in labelling theory may be warranted as an important adjunct to a critical Sociology-of-Law analysis of youth crime and justice.

chapter seven

Cultural Perception and

Mainstream Law

One of the foci of this book is the influence that the race/ethnicity of a young offender has on the treatment that the offender receives in the Canadian youth justice system. In this chapter, I hope to convey some of the reasons why the law has such difficulty in administering impartial justice. Although the discussions are somewhat philosophical, they do address the fundamental origins of bias in the legal system, especially as it pertains to Native youths. I would add, however, that the problems of jurisprudence discussed in this chapter are experienced not only by Native youths, but also by any young offender who experiences the justice system as foreign and intimidating. Such offenders might come from other ethnic and racial groups, from lower classes with different linguistic and educational skills, and from youth groups who do not adapt well to the world of adults.

In previous chapters, I argued that Native youth react differently to social control, are perceived differently by social control agents, and have different legal experiences than their non-Native counterparts. The reasons for this are complex. They involve not only racial stereotyping by the legal system, but also conflicting cultural norms between Native culture and the law, which is primarily staffed by relatively high-status, White legal practitioners. The modern legal system is very much based on formal rules of conduct and procedure. The rigidity of law and its authoritative structure are functional requirements for the smooth operation of the legal system. Ironically, it may be this rigidity and the adherence to the principles of equality before the law that contribute to disparities in legal treatment. The following discussion of how Native culture stands at variance to legal culture illustrates why the 'impartial rule of law' philosophy of the legal system is not effective or fair in dealing with youth who do not hold to the values which underpin jurisprudence, and it helps explain the disparities in justice experienced by Native youths.

I look to several noteworthy sources to inform my discussion. Rupert Ross has authored a compelling study on Native culture and the legal system entitled *Dancing with the Ghost: Exploring Indian Reality* (1992). Ross's study of the Ojibway and Cree people of Ontario vividly illustrates why the Native world view places Native people at a disadvantage in an essentially foreign legal system. I turn also to Carol LaPrairie's work on Native youth in Northern courts (LaPrairie 1988; 1983) and to the Law Reform Commission of Canada report entitled *Aboriginal Peoples and Criminal Justice* (1991). These works, among others, outline the incompatibility of conventional jurisprudence with Aboriginal cultural practices and values.

It would be a mistake, however, to assume that Native culture in Canada is monolithic. Certainly cultural and social control practices vary widely depending on tribal background and historical development. On the other hand, many common cultural practices that stem from similar historical, geographical, and subsistence exigencies do exist and are identifiable, especially in contradistinction with the normative practices of Canada's legal system. The resulting disparities are primarily an indication of the inability of a rigid Euro-Canadian legal system to accommodate difference. In addition, the court itself is a place that is foreign to most lay people, irrespective of their ethnic and cultural background. The formal rules of court, the authority structure, the language of law, and the informal rules that facilitate the process of justice are unfamiliar to all but a few insiders. The court appears to place both offender and victim outside the process; only those with educational and financial resources can force entry back in. The accused and the victim are essentially disenfranchised from the process of justice, and their plight is given over to lawyers and judges whose function is 'administration'. Let us examine how Native culture stands in contrast to and in conflict with legal culture.

The Misreading of Signs

When two cultures meet, the misreading of verbal and physical signs constitutes a primary obstacle to mutual accommodation, especially in the context of legal disputes. For example, Ross (1992) illustrates that silence or a reluctance to verbalize, which is typical of many Native peoples, is at odds with the requirements of courtroom procedure and is often viewed by justice officials as indifference or defiance. The explanation for such behaviour in many cases is rooted in a system of ethics and traditions which stresses the private resolution of conflict. In the spirit of the Young Offenders Act, however, the individual youth is asked, now more than ever, to proactively present his or her case in an adversarial (and confrontational) manner. This legal requirement stands at odds with traditional Native stoicism.

Furthermore, cultural and legal customs collide when body language is misinterpreted as disrespect. The customary respect required in legal contexts involves standing in a rigid fashion and focusing on the judge and court offi-cials, especially when they are speaking. Ross suggests that for many Native cultures, looking someone straight in the eye is disrespectful, and that looking away, especially downward, is considered a sign of respect; being looked in the eye is intimidating. Non-native peoples have been socialized to read looking away as a sign of evasiveness or indifference, and nowhere is this misreading of signals more evident than in juvenile courts where judicial officials demand deference and view ostensible inattention as a confrontational posture. The examples of eye contact and silence illustrate quite clearly how cultural signals can be misinterpreted by both sides in a legal confrontation. The mutual stress and anger that results exacerbate the inability of the court to bilaterally resolve many young offenders' cases. And, of course, the mere lack of life- and legal-experiences characteristic of all young offenders further disadvantages them when confronted by adults.

These two specific examples illustrate that, at a more general level, Native culture and legal culture are based on fundamentally different philosophical premises. Here we see most clearly the essential insolubility of the problems that confront Native youth in non-Native legal systems. The Law Reform Commis-sion of Canada in its review entitled *Aboriginal Peoples and Criminal Justice* summarizes the cultural collision between Native individuals from isolated communities and the legal system:

> From the Aboriginal perspective, the criminal justice system is an alien one, imposed by the dominant white society. Wherever they turn or are shuttled throughout the system, Aboriginal offenders, victims or witnesses encounter a sea of white faces. Not surprisingly, they regard the system as deeply insensitive to their traditions and values: many view it as unremittingly racist.... For those living in remote and reserve communities, the entire court apparatus, quite literally, appears to descend from the sky—an impression that serves to magnify their feelings of isolation and erects barriers to their attaining an understanding of the system. (1991: 5)

Native versus Legal Culture

The general principles that divide Native and legal culture include (a) the right and the necessity of accusing the accuser, (b) the need and the right to pursue self-defence aggressively, and (c) the importance of time and punctuality to the smooth running of the court system. In the first instance, the fundamental adversarial right that accrues to defendants stands at variance with Native traditions regarding non-interference. Ross describes the ethic of non-interference from the perspective of Mohawk psychiatrist Dr Clare Brant: 'We are very loath to confront people. We are very loath to give advice to anyone if the person is not specifically asking for advice. To interfere or even comment on their behaviour is considered rude' (1992:13). Giving evidence in defence of self or others is essential to the confrontational style of the court system, but it is considered a moral violation for Native culture. Young offenders who have been taught the ethic of non-interference or who have merely grown up within this cultural tradition are used to reticence; such reticence is misinterpreted by legal officials.

Secondly, the fundamental legal right aggressively to pursue self-defence involves, in most court cases, reasoned and emotional responses to accusation. Anger and indignance, then, become effective postures for both the defendant and his or her counsel. Despite the rationality of the court system, impassioned pleas do have influence and are best served in a context of accusation. As in the case of the ethic of non-interference, however, Native cultural norms prohibit the besting or the embarrassing of others (or at least not being openly victorious). Such behaviour mitigates against making accusation. It is difficult to imagine how the typical Native young offender, if he or she holds to the principle of not disgracing others, could experience success in an adversarial system that demands that others be bested or at least embarrassed. Furthermore, the Native ethic of not expressing anger, which is well-documented by Ross (1992), is part of the prohibition against burdening others. From a Native cultural perspective, anger violates the well-being of those who are its targets, and the suppression of anger and other emotions is a condition of rightness and fairness. Consider this posture in the context of the average court where victory is the end and aggression is the means. At a more general/philosophical level, the notion of victory which is obviously fundamental to legal battles is neither desirable nor acceptable for many Native offenders because winning implies diminishing others.

Ross illustrates quite clearly how the suppression of emotion can be constructed or misconstrued as unhealthy at the least, or pathological at best:

A young Native offender was brought into court one day to be sentenced on a number of serious charges that involved explosions of violence and vandalism while he was intoxicated. It was clear that this young man had many unresolved emotional problems for he had been constantly in trouble with the law and had already been placed in a number of different institutions. That formed a part of the court's dilemma, for we wanted to find a place that showed the greatest promise of involving him in some successful therapy. We spent a considerable amount of time talking about what he needed when he suddenly interrupted our discussion. He said that he'd been through different kinds of therapy already but that it didn't work. Therapy would fail, he said, not because he was embarrassed to talk about them, but because it wasn't right to talk about them. It wasn't right to 'burden' other people in that way. Once again, we get a glimpse into a strong conflict between two notions of what is 'right'.

In the mainstream culture we are virtually bombarded with magazine articles, books and television talk shows telling us how to delve into our psyches, how to explore our deepest griefs and neuroses, how to talk about them, get them out in the open, share them, and so on. At times it seems as if the person who can't find a treatable neurosis deep within himself must for that reason alone be really neurotic!

The Native exhortation, however, seems to go in the opposite direction. It is fully consistent with rules against criticism and advice-giving, because it forbids the burdening of others. It is almost as if speaking about your worries puts an obligation on others to both share and respond, an obligation difficult to meet, given the prohibition against offering advice in return.

Even the act of concentrating privately on your feelings seems to be discouraged. Such self-indulgence seems to be viewed as a further source of possible debilitation which poses a threat to the survival of the group.

As a Crown Attorney, I regularly receive psychiatric assessments of Native people in trouble with the law. They invariably say something like, 'This Native person refuses to address his psychological difficulties and instead retreats into denial and silence when pressed.' Such reports are often full of words like 'unresponsive', 'undemonstrative', 'uncommunicative' and the like. The final word is 'uncooperative', with all the negative inferences such a word implies. Of course he refuses to 'cooperate', to pour out his innermost thoughts and feelings. For many hundred of years, that is what his people taught was the proper thing to do.

I suspect that the number of psychiatric mis-diagnoses of Native people must be staggering, for we cannot see their behaviour except through our own eyes, our own notions of propriety. To us, the person who refuses to dig deep within his psyche and then divulge all that he sees is someone with serious psychological problems. At the very least, he is someone who, we conclude, has no interest in coming to grips with his difficulties, no interest in trying to turn his life around. That conclusion leaves the court with long deterrent jail sentences, rather than rehabilitation, as the only apparent option. . . . Unable to see beyond our own ways we fail to see that there are others, and we draw negative conclusions about the 'refusal' or 'failure' or 'inability' of other people to use our mode of behaviour. (Ross 1992: 32-4)

This passage illustrates that the legal misinterpretation of stoicism as indifference or defiance is compounded by the medical profession which uses behaviour as a means of diagnosing mental disorder. When psychiatry and the law intersect in the control of youth misconduct, the possibilities for cultural insensitivity appear endless. At a more philosophical level, the Native concept of healing as both spiritual and holistic is at variance with the psychiatric/medical model, which stresses individual pathology, with special emphasis on diagnosis and labelling.

The third concept that divides Native and non-Native culture in legal cases is time. In a rational, time-dependent society, adherence to schedules is important to the operation of bureaucracies. The court system especially works most efficiently when space and time are rigidly allocated. Furthermore, in a non-Native context, we attach negative labels such as tardiness, undependability, and disrespect to those who violate the ethic of punctuality. And of course we become angry when people do not show up on time. This is the cultural context of the court, and it stands in contrast to Native culture in which time is understood differently. It is not that time is unimportant in Native culture, rather that time cannot be forced. The 'time must be right' philosophy is essentially one in which things unfold naturally and that conflict cannot be resolved until the natural course of events has taken place. Quite clearly courts need to force resolution, and often the courts misinterpret lateness as disrespect for the court system and its officials. As Ross argues, the 'time is right philosophy' is neither mystical nor capricious. Rather, it is a practical approach to the solution of problems in which success can be obtained when practically possible. The Native youth in court, when faced with a rigid clock-oriented system that rewards punctuality and expediency, is arguably disadvantaged.

In the last section of this chapter, I wish to discuss two final issues surrounding Native culture which have rather substantial influences on the type of justice that is meted out to Native youth: Native family structure and Native spirituality. Both are directly connected to the discussion on time and problem solution.

Native Family Structure

A central focus of the court-based research in this book is the influence of family structure on judicial decisions, either indirectly through justice officials' perceptions of the stability of certain families, or directly through the influence that parents or guardians have on the processing of youth. The Euro-centric legal assumption in this regard is that parents will take an active role in seeking justice for their children and that they will be responsible for the future conduct of the child. Section 10 of the Young Offenders Act explicitly states that parents who fail to be present in court are liable for contempt of court and summary conviction (see Appendix I). As well, the results of this book's court data analysis indicate quite clearly that youths who are accompanied by parents or guardians are much more successful in accessing justice. For many Native families, however, the legal cultural expectations of family involvement contradict Native cultural practice.

Firstly, in many Native communities, children are given much greater autonomy than in non-Native communities. The ethic of non-interference, even in the lives of offspring, appears to many legal and social services individuals to be an inappropriate child-rearing technique. When these individuals, in the spirit of the Young Offenders Act, make recommendations and judgements regarding the future of Native youth, they do so in the belief that any child left to his or her own devices is necessarily being neglected. As Ross argues, this is not inevitably the case:

> Our child care workers, through no fault of their own, regularly see behaviour which, to them, is a clear signal of lack of parental concern. When they see children consistently left to their devices, apparently free of adult supervision and control, they cannot help but be drawn towards the conclusion that nobody cares. When that conclusion is joined with other culture-specific judgements such as over-crowding (and there is a painful shortage of houses in most communities), the temptation to put the matter before the courts is strong; their duty, after all, requires that they do exactly that when they see a child who, in the words of the legislation, is 'in need of protection'. If, within the other culture, however, care and concern are demonstrated in different fashions, such a conclusion may well be false. (1992: 18-19)

LaPrairie (1988) argues in this respect that the Young Offenders Act, in its attempts to ensure parental suitability for supervision upon release, uses socio-cultural factors like parental employment status, structure of the family, income, and community factors in its decisions. Where the courts have the discretion to place young offenders in the care of suitable adults [see Appendix I, YOA 3(1)(h), 7, 8], they do so on the basis of perceptions that are distinctly at odds with Native parenting practice.

Secondly, it is likely that Native, traditional child-rearing practices do present problems for Native kids in an unfamiliar world where children may be in need of relatively constant protection. In many cases, children from Northern communities leave home to pursue educational opportunities and are forced to confront a world where their autonomy from their families is a liability. This is nowhere more apparent than in schools and courts where parental absence is misinterpreted as neglect. Traditional communities are not without internal problems, however. Those problems are becoming somewhat commonplace in Native communities. York's work (1991) on Native land claims describes the devastating effects of industrial intrusion into northern communities. Here we see the transformation, in a matter of years, of once vital traditional communities into disorganized societies where crime and substance abuse are epidemic. As York (1991) argues, the development of natural resources has resulted in the transplanting of subsistence societies (and the relinquishing of land claims) whose material and social resources have been depleted or altered. Ross describes how this industrial transformation creates a 'numbing idleness' for which, especially for youth, there is no escape: 'The families that once expended formidable daily effort just to survive now have virtually nothing to do, nothing to accomplish, nothing to find satisfaction in' (1992: 117). As a result, Native parents are caught in the vortex of a major cultural devolution, and they are frustrated and ill-prepared to deal with children who are now faced with constricted opportunities for work and expanded opportunities for getting into trouble. I might add, as well, that children have a great propensity to internalize the society around them as it is presented through the fiction of television. In the modern world the traditional Native ethic of childhood autonomy becomes both a practical and a legal liability.

LaPrairie (1988) identifies the practical social and legal problems that Native families experience in northern communities and describes the 'welfare ghetto' that has resulted from colonization and discriminatory, culturally insensitive development. The community is no longer the steadying influence that it once was in Native areas. The countervailing forces of industrialization have created a situation in which Native youths are not only alienated and despairing, but also rebellious and anti-social. All of this occurs in geographical isolation from mainstream society, resulting in two major implications for Native youth. Firstly, hinterland resource areas tend to be difficult places to live, and the economies are erratic and temporary. Single-industry resource towns, for example, are notoriously unpleasant places to live, and unfortunately dependent on the whim of one volatile resource market. As LaPrairie (1988) argues, the social disorganization of these communities directly affects justice as administered by the Young Offenders Act. The development and use of community alternatives, the provision of employment opportunities—which in many cases affect pre-disposition reports and dispositions, the ability of parents to attend court and to provide alternatives to custody, and the presence and affordability of counsel are all diminished in marginal communities. Secondly, geographic isolation dictates that justice is administered by outsiders. When this occurs, not only are the quality and the availability of services low (Kueneman *et al.* 1983), but also justice workers, who generally do not have a social or cultural interest in the communities and who are often overworked, tend to administer justice 'by the book'. As a result, essentially foreign systems of justice like the Young Offenders Act are not administered with the culturally-sensitive discretion that would be needed to make them more just.

Native Spirituality and the Law

The final discussion in this chapter involves the connection between spirituality and legal practice. Again, we see cultural collision. In a Judeo-Christian-based institution swearing on the bible symbolizes both a legal and a spiritually binding commitment to tell the truth. Furthermore, many of the philosophical premises of justice such as reparation, compensation, and grievance are remnants of 'an eye for an eye', Old Testament morality. Most importantly, the practice of the courts in judging past behaviour and asking for remorse and contrition is clearly connected to the influence of mainstream Judeo-Christian religion. Ironically, Native spirituality, which directs and underscores Native cultural values and practices, is philosophically opposed to the aforementioned tenets of legal culture. The courts require sanctity, but only of a certain kind. Ross's final chapter in *Dancing with a Ghost* illustrates how Native spirituality is present-oriented and does not dwell on guilt or past grievances. Because the human being is naturally close to the creator, indiscretions, mistakes, or criminal violations are, as a result, handled with positive coaxing instead of guilt and punishment. Ross replies to those who object to this contention:

> Could it be that we view people as being defined not by essential strength and goodness but by weakness and, if not outright malevolence, then at least indifference to others? Our judicial lectures and religious sermons seem to dwell on how hard we will have to work not to give in to our base instincts. Is that how we see ourselves, and each other?
>
> Whether that is accurate or not as a general proposition, the Elders of Sandy Lake (and elsewhere) certainly do not speak from within that sort of perspective. At every step they tell each offender they meet with not about how hard he'll have to work to control his base self but instead how they are there to help him realize the goodness that is within him.
>
> In short, the Elders seem to do their best to convince people that they are one step away from heaven instead of one step away from hell. They define their role not within anything remotely like the doctrine of original sin but within another, diametrically opposite doctrine which I will call the doctrine of original sanctity.
>
> Sceptics can argue that what I am talking about here is a distinction without substance, an argument with no more significance than the philosopher's debate

about whether a glass of water is half-full or half-empty. I do not think that is the case, I think the difference between the two emphases is critical.

The freely chosen responses to criminal activity illustrate the differences which flow from adopting each of the two perspectives. If it is your conviction that people live one short step from hell, that it is more natural to sin than to do good, then your response as a judicial official will be to use terror to prevent the taking of that last step backward. You will be quick to threaten offenders with dire consequences should they 'slide back' into their destructive ways. In fact, a band councillor once asked me directly why our courts came into his community when all we wanted to do was, in his words, 'terrorize my people with jail and fines'. If, by contrast, it is your conviction that people live one step away from heaven, you will be more likely to respond by coaxing them gently forward, by encouraging them to progress, to realize the goodness within them. The use of coercion, threats or punishment by those who would serve as guides to goodness would seem a denial of the very vision that inspires them. And that, I suggest, is how elders see it. (1992: 168-9)

This long passage illustrates, I think, the fundamental characteristic that undermines the civil rights of First Nations peoples in the court system. The Native offender who is imbued with a rather positive, future-oriented philosophy comes face to face with a legal philosophy preoccupied with the past and one that demands the admission of guilt and the promise of reparation. Section 4 (1e and 2a) of the Young Offenders Act clearly states that for leniency—in the form of alternative measures—to be given, the offender must admit participation or involvement in the offence. The denial of guilt becomes, then, a reason for harsher treatment. Furthermore, nowhere is the legal philosophy more apparent than in the use of previous record and predisposition reports to make judicial decisions. The assumption here is that the character of the individual can be constructed from the past and that future goodness can be discerned from past indiscretions. As labelling theorists have argued, however, any social control agent can gather enough negative things about any citizen to create a biography that would be legally damning. As we can see from the Young Offenders Act, Section 14 (Appendix I) and the court analysis in Chapter Six, the use of past criminal behaviour and the use of negative dossiers are deemed to be important in law and have a substantial impact on the outcome of justice. Ross (1992) argues, however, that the legal philosophy is in fundamental opposition to Native spirituality; court philosophy assumes that future acts will likely be bad, while Native philosophy assumes that future acts will be good. It is here, I believe, where the Native young offender is fundamentally disadvantaged by legal culture.

In this book, I am arguing that the youth justice system in Canada is applied with discrimination. This chapter is important because it illustrates how the clash between different cultural philosophies can result in the unfair administration of justice. While not all Native and other minority Canadian youth are complete cultural strangers to the courts, the fact remains that many children raised with certain cultural and ethnic values are at a distinct legal disadvantage because those values contradict the rigid legal values of the Canadian courts.

chapter eight

Conclusions

I deliberated for a considerable length of time on how to end this book. Initially, I considered summarizing the results of the analysis in the context of social policy and law reform, with the intention of analysing those areas of the Young Offenders Act which exacerbate the problem of youth crime. I abandoned that approach, firstly because the answers can be realized from the arguments in this book; secondly, because the exercise of social policy advocacy, while potentially helpful, implies that answers are simple and attainable within the confines of jurisprudence. Quite clearly, this is not the case.

Many of the youth who come into contact with the law, especially for the first time, are victims themselves, whether victims of family violence, privation, or discrimination. I address the reader to a compelling and passionate study by Marlene Webber entitled *Street Kids: The Tragedy of Canada's Runaways*. To compound the difficulty, the legal system in general is not accessible for the majority of citizens. The language of the law, the rules of order and conduct, and the informal machinations between lawyers and judges are all instances in which the offender is an outsider. I would argue, as well, that youth are doubly disadvantaged because the courtroom is also an adult world as well as a legal world.

Marlene Webber's series of case studies of the lives of runaway youths in Canada describes the constant victimization in the lives of children who are risk with the law. Many of the youth she discusses were victims of sexual and other forms of physical abuse as young children. She argues that they are emotionally, socially, and occupationally unprepared to assume life in the adult world. Prostitution and drug use are the norm, and both high-risk activities are exploited by pimps and pushers at great cost to the youth. Most importantly in

Webber's work, I believe, is the implicit suggestion that these youths are socially and legally 'trapped on the street'. The police and courts deal very legalistically with street youths; their impersonal, formalistic posture seems to exacerbate the problems of poverty and victimization. Simply put, the system of law and order cannot possibly deal with the problems that high-risk youths face. The problems are structural and, while they are manifested at the individual/psychological level, they seem to be insurmountable. Such futility leads one to think that the only way of addressing the social and legal problems that many youths face is to abandon the system of legality and accountability and reinstitute something more akin to the welfare model of the Juvenile Delinquency Act of 1908. Unfortunately, the Juvenile Delinquency Act child welfare perspective on youth in trouble with the law became a vehicle for the excessive use of discretion and, as a consequence, was directed largely against susceptible youths.

Before I suggest a way out of the dilemma of 'nothing works', I would briefly like to comment on my second point, that the legal system, at present, is minimally accessible for most people and even less so for adolescents. The threatening and foreign nature of the court cannot be underestimated. Much of the legal procedure occurs in the absence of the accused. If he or she is present, the procedure is minimally explained or understood. Exclusion is compounded by legal language that is not understandable even by the well-educated. Ericson and Baranek have argued that the justice system is constructed to exclude the accused and to facilitate the operation of the control system. They maintain that 'the criminal process is designed so that it does not give the accused more rights than would upset the operation of criminal control in the interests of the state' (1986: 47). The accused, furthermore, does not have access to the 'recipe' of knowledge and language that facilitates the system and he or she is relatively ineffective in influencing the administration of justice. Quite clearly, the legal and organizational rules are used to process people primarily through findings of guilt, and to simplify the jobs of administrators and legal agents.

Whether one assumes a political economic approach or a more organizational approach to the study of the bureaucratic nature of justice, it appears that the accused is a marginal player. I would add, as I have argued throughout this book, that members of certain cultural and language groups are doubly marginalized by the courts. The Manitoba Aboriginal Justice Inquiry (1991) has quite clearly articulated the problems that Native peoples encounter in courts, especially problems dealing with language difference and conflicting cultural and legal norms. The Report of the Saskatchewan Indian Justice Review Committee (Linn 1991), spelling out the need for interpretive services in court and the need for young Aboriginal offenders to be able to access elders, also has argued the inappropriateness of legal culture for many people and the hope that intervention strategies can embody holistic, culturally appropriate approaches to the rehabilitation of Native young offenders. I would add that the courts must employ strategies that are sensitive to *all* youth as legal strangers; formalized, legalistic court practices and procedures are inappropriate for addressing structural issues that are at the core of youth crime.

The message of this book is not all doom and gloom. The essential strategies for ensuring justice for young people in Canada seem relatively clear. The foremost strategy must be based on a sensitivity to young offenders as victims first and offenders secondly and consequently. If we do not constantly publicize and incorporate victimization into our justice system, we are bound to fall into the abyss of 'lock-'em-up' justice which doubly victimizes young offenders. Secondly, we must be aware that the court is an ethnocentric 'culture' making stereotypical judgements that are often incorrect and harmful. Strategies must be found to remove justice from traditional, past-focused jurisprudence into the realm of holistic, future-focused resolve. While these strategies sound idealistic, I believe they have the potential to address the structural roots of youth misconduct as well as the traditional, legal roots of unfair and discriminatory justice.

Appendix I

Policy for Canada with respect to young offenders—Act to be liberally constructed.

3. (1)It is hereby recognized and declared that

(a) while young persons should not in all instances be held accountable in the same manner or suffer the same consequences for their behaviour as adults, young persons who commit offences should nonetheless bear responsibility for their contraventions;

(b) society must, although it has the responsibility to take reasonable measures to prevent criminal conduct by young persons, be afforded the necessary protection from illegal behaviour;

(c) young persons who commit offences require supervision, discipline and control, but, because of their state of dependency and level of development and maturity, they also have special needs and require guidance and assistance;

(d) where it is not inconsistent with the protection of society, taking no measures of taking measures other than judicial proceedings under this Act should be considered for dealing with young persons who have committed offences;

(e) young persons have rights and freedoms in their own right including those stated in the *Canadian Charter of Rights and Freedoms or in the Canadian Bill of Rights*, and in particular a right to be heard in the course of, and to participate in, the processes that lead to decisions that affect them, and young persons should have special guarantees of their rights and freedoms;

(f) in the application of this Act, the rights and freedoms of young persons include a right to the least possible interference with freedom that is consistent with the protection of society, having regard to the needs of young persons and the interests of their families;

(g) young persons have the right, in every instance where they have rights of freedoms that may be affected by this Act, to be informed as to what those rights and freedoms are; and

(h) parents have responsibility for the care and supervision of their children, and, for that reason, young persons should be removed from parental supervision either partly or entirely only when measures that provide for continuing parental supervision are inappropriate.

(2) This Act shall be liberally constructed to the end that young persons will be dealt with in accordance with the principles set out in subsection (1).

ALTERNATIVE MEASURES

Alternative Measures—Restriction on use—Admissions not admissible in evidence—No bar to proceedings—Laying of information, etc.

4. (1) Alternative measures may be used to deal with a young person alleged to have committed an offence instead of judicial proceedings under this Act only if

(a) the measures are part of a program of alternative measures authorized by the Attorney General or his delegate or authorized by a person, or a person within a class of persons, designated by the Lieutenant Governor in Council of a province;

(b) the person who is considering whether to use such measures is satisfied that they would be appropriate, having regard to the needs of the young persons and the interests of society;

(c) the young person, having been informed of the alternative measure, fully and freely consents to participate therein;

(d) the young person has, before consenting to participate in the alternative measures, been advised of his right to be represented by counsel and been given a reasonable opportunity to consult with counsel;

(e) the young person accepts responsibility for the act or omission that forms the basis of the offence that he is alleged to have committed;

(f) there is, in the opinion of the Attorney General or his agent, sufficient evidence to proceed with the prosecution of the offence; and

(g) the prosecution of the offence is not in any way barred at law.

(2) Alternative measures shall not be used to deal with a young person alleged to have committed an offence if the young person

(a) denies his participation or involvement in the commission of the offence; or

(b) expresses his wishes to have any charge against him dealt with by the youth court.

(3) No admission, confession or statement accepting responsibility for a given act or omission made by a young person alleged to have committed an offence as a condition of his being dealt with by alternative measures shall be admissible in evidence against him in any civil or criminal proceedings.

(4) The use of alterative measures in respect of a young person alleged to have committed an offence is not a bar to proceedings against him under this Act, but

(a) where the youth court is satisfied on a balance of probabilities that the young person has totally complied with the terms and conditions of the alternative measures, the youth court shall dismiss any charge against him; and

(b) where the youth court is satisfied on a balance of probabilities that the young person has partially complied with the terms and conditions of the alternative measures, the youth court may dismiss any charge against him if, in the opinion of the court, the prosecution of the charge would, having regard to the circumstances, be unfair, and the youth court may consider the young person's performance with respect to the alternative measures before making a disposition under this Act.

(5) Subject to subsection (4), nothing in this section shall be constructed to prevent any person from laying an information, obtaining the issue or confirmation of any process of proceeding with the prosecution of any offence in accordance with the law.

There is no requirement that the authorities consider alternative measures in the case of every young offender. Further the offender is not entitled to a hearing and an opportunity to participate in and be heard when the authorities are in fact considering such measures: Re T.W. and THE QUEEN (1986),

25 C.C.C. (3d) 89 (Sask. Q.B.). Contra: R. v. J.B. (1985), 20 C.C.C. (3d) 67 (B.C. Prov. Ct.) where it was held that the young person is entitled to notice and to be present and represented by counsel when the authorities are considering alternative measures under this section.

DETENTION PRIOR TO DISPOSITION

Designated place of temporary detention—Exception—Detention separate from adults—Transfer by provincial director—Exception relating to temporary detention—Authorization of provincial authority for detention—Determination by provincial authority of place of detention.

7. (1) A young person who is

(a) arrested and detained prior to the making of a disposition in respect of the young person under section 20, or

(b) detained pursuant to a warrant issued under subsection 32(6) shall, subject to subsection (4), be detained in a place of temporary detention designated as such by the Lieutenant Governor in Council of the appropriate province of his delegate or in a place within a class of such places so designated.

(1.1) A young person who is detained in a place of temporary detention pursuant to subsection (1) may, in the course of being transferred from that place to the court or from the court to that place, be held under the supervision and control of a peace officer.

(2) A young person referred to in subsection (1) shall be held separate and apart from any adult who is detained or held in custody unless a youth court judge or a justice is satisfied that

(a) the young person cannot, having regard to his own safety or the safety of others, be detained in a place of detention for young persons; or

(b) no place of detention for young persons is available within a reasonable distance.

(3) A young person who is detained in custody in accordance with subsection (1) may, during the period of detention, be transferred by the provincial director from one place of temporary detention to another.

PLACEMENT OF YOUNG PERSON IN CARE OF RESPONSIBLE PERSON—Condition of placement—Removing young person from care—Order—Effect of arrest.

7.1 (1)Where a youth court judge or a justice is satisfied that

(a) a young person who has been arrested would, but for this subsection, be detained in custody.

(b) a responsible person is willing and able to take care of and exercise control over the young person, and

(c) the young person is willing to be placed in the care of that person the young person may be placed in the care of that person instead of being detained in custody.

(2) A young person shall not be placed in the care of a person under subsection (1) unless

(a) that person undertakes in writing to take care of and to be responsible for the attendance of the young person in court when required and to comply with such other conditions as the youth court judge of justice may specify; and

(b) the young person undertakes in writing to comply with the arrangement and to comply with such other conditions as the youth court judge or justice may specify.

(3) Where a young person has been placed in the care of a person under subsection (1) and

(a) that person is no longer willing or able to take care of or exercise control over the young person, or

(b) it is, for any other reason, no longer appropriate that the young person be placed in the care of that person, the young person, the person in whose care the young person has been placed or any other person may, by application in writing to a youth court judge or a justice, apply for an order under subsection (4).

(4) Where a youth court judge or a justice is satisfied that a young person should not remain in custody of the person in whose care he was placed under subsection (1), the youth court judge or justice shall

(a) make an order relieving the person and the young person of the obligations undertaken pursuant to subsection (2); and

(b) issue a warrant for the arrest of the young person.

(5) Where a young person is arrested pursuant to a warrant issued under paragraph (4)(b), the young person shall be taken before a youth court judge or justice forthwith and dealt with under section 457 of the *Criminal Code.* 1986, c. 32, s. 5.

APPLICATION TO YOUTH COURT—Notice to prosecutor—Notice to young person—Waiver of notice—Application for review under section 457.5 or 457.6 of *Criminal Code*—Idem—Interim by youth court judge only—Reviewed by court of appeal.

8. (1)[Repealed. 1986, c. 32, s. 6.]

(2) Where an order is made under section 457 of the *Criminal Code* in respect of a young person by a justice who is not a youth court judge, an application may, at any time after the order is made, be made to a youth court for the release from or detention in custody of the young person, as the case may be, and the youth court shall hear the matter as an original application.

(3) An application under subsection (2) for release from custody shall not be heard unless the young person has given the prosecutor at least two clear days notice in writing of the application.

(4) An application under subsection (2) for detention in custody shall not be heard unless the prosecutor has given the young person at least two days notice in writing of the application.

(5) The requirement for a notice under subsection (3) or (4) may be waived by the prosecutor or by the young person or his council, as the case may be.

NOTICES TO PARENTS

Notice to parents in case of arrest—Notice to parent in case of summons or appearance notice—Notice to relative or other adult—Notice to spouse—Notice on direction of youth court judge or justice—Contents of notice—Service of notice—Proceedings not invalid—Exception—Where a notice not served.

9. (1) Subject to subsections (3) and (4), where a young person is arrested and detained in custody pending his appearance in court, the officer in charge at the time the young person is detained shall, as soon as possible, give or cause to be given, orally or in writing, to a parent of the young person notice of the arrest stating the place of detention and the reason for the arrest.

(2) Subject to subsections (3) and (4), where a summons or an appearance notice is issued in respect of a young person, the person who issued the summons or appearance notice, or, where a young person is released on giving his promise to appear or entering into a recognizance, the officer in charge shall as soon as possible, give cause to be given, in writing, to a parent of the young person notice of the summons, appearance notice, promise to appear or recognizance.

(3) Where the whereabouts of the parents of a young person

(a) who is arrested and detained in custody,

(b) in respect of whom a summons or an appearance notice is issued, or

(c) who is released on giving his promise to appear or entering into a recognizance

are not known or it appears that no parent is available, a notice under this section may be given to an adult relative of the young person who is known to the young person and is likely to assist him or, if no such adult relative is available, to such other adult who is known to the young person and is likely to assist him as the person giving the notice considers appropriate.

(4) Where a young person described in paragraph (3)(a), (b) or (c) is married, a notice under this section may be given to the spouse of the young person instead of a parent.

(5) Where doubt exists as to the person to whom a notice under this section should be given, a youth court judge or, where a youth court judge is, having regard to the circumstances, not reasonably available, a justice may give directions as to the person to whom the notice should be given, in accordance with such directions is sufficient notice for the purposes of this section.

Order Requiring Attendance of Parent—Service of order—Failure to attend—Appeal—Warrant to arrest parent.

10. (1) Where a parent does not attend proceedings before a youth court in respect of a young person, the court may, if in its opinion the presence of the parent is necessary or in the best interest of the young person, by ordering in writing require the parent to attend at any stage of the proceedings.

(2) A copy of any order made under subsection (1) shall be served by a peace officer or by a person designated by a youth court by delivering it personally to the parent to whom it is directed, unless the youth court authorizes service by registered mail.

(3) A parent who is ordered to attend a youth court pursuant to subsection (1) and who fails without reasonable excuse, the proof of which lies on that parent, to comply with the order

(a) is guilty of contempt of court; and

(b) may be dealt with summarily by the court; and

(c) is liable to the punishment provided for in the *Criminal Code* for a summary conviction offence.

(5) If a parent who is ordered to attend a youth court pursuant to subsection (1) does not attend at the time and place named in the order or fails to remain in attendance as required and it is proved that a copy of the order was served on the parent, a youth court may issue a warrant to compel the attendance of the parent. 1986, c. 32, s. 8.

RIGHT TO COUNSEL

Right to retain counsel—Arresting officer to advise young person of right to counsel—Justice, youth court or review board to advise young person of right to counsel—Trial, hearing or review before youth court or review board—Appointment of counsel—Release hearing before justice—Young person may be assisted by adult—Counsel independent of parents—Statement of right to counsel.

11. (1) A young person has the right to retain and instruct counsel without delay, and to exercise that right personally, at any stage of proceedings against the young person and prior to and during any consideration of whether, instead of commencing or continuing judicial proceedings against the young person under this Act, to use alternative measures to deal with the young person.

(2) Every young person who is arrested or detained shall, forthwith on his arrest of detention, be advised by the arresting office or the officer in charge, as the case may be, of his right to be represented by counsel and shall be given an opportunity to obtain counsel.

(3) Where a young person is not represented by counsel

(a) at a hearing at which it will be determined whether to release the young person or detain him in custody prior to disposition of his case,

(b) at a hearing held pursuant to section 16,

(c) at his trial, or

(d) at a review of a disposition held before a youth court or a review board under this Act, the justice before whom, or the youth court or review board before which, the hearing, trial or review is held shall advise the young person of his right to be represented by counsel and shall give the young person a reasonable opportunity to obtain counsel.

(4) Where a young person at his trial or at a hearing or review referred to in subsection (3) wishes to obtain counsel but is unable to do so, the youth court before which the hearing, trial or review is held or the review board before which the review is held

(a) shall, where there is a legal aid or assistance program available in the province where the hearing, trial or review is held, refer the young person to that program for the appointment of counsel; or

(b) where no legal aid or assistance program is available or the young person is unable to obtain counsel through such program, may, and on the request of the young person shall, direct that the young person be represented by counsel.

(5) Where a direction is made under paragraph (4)(b) in respect of a young person, the Attorney General of the province in which the direction is made shall appoint counsel, or cause counsel to be appointed, to represent the young person.

(6) Where a young person at a hearing before a justice who is not a youth court judge at which it will be determined whether to release the young person or detain him in custody prior to disposition of his case wishes to obtain counsel but is unable to do so, the justice shall

(a) where there is a legal aid or assistance program available in the province where the hearing is held,

(i) refer the young person to that program for the appointment of counsel, or

(ii) refer the matter to a youth court to be dealt with in accordance with paragraph (4)(a) or (b); or

(b) where no legal aid or assistance program is available or the young person is unable to obtain counsel through such program, refer the matter to a youth court to be dealt with in accordance with paragraph (4)(b).

(7) Where a young person is not represented by counsel at his trial or at a hearing or review referred to in subsection (3), the justice before whom or the youth court or review board before which the proceedings are held may, on the request of the young person, allow the young person to be assisted by an adult whom the justice, court or review board considers to be suitable.

(8) In any case where it appears to a youth court judge or a justice that the interests of a young person and his parents are in conflict or that it would be in the best interest of the young person to be represented by his own counsel, the judge or justice shall ensure that the young person is represented by counsel independent of his parents.

(9) A statement that a young person has the right to be represented by counsel shall be included in any appearance notice or summons issued to the young person, any warrant to arrest the young person, any promise to

appear given by the young person, any recognizance entered into before an officer in charge by the young person or any notice of a review of a disposition given to the young person. 1986, c. 32, s. 9.

APPEARANCE

Where young person appears—Waiver—Where young person not represented by counsel—Where youth court not satisfied.

12. (1) Where a young person against whom an information is laid first appears before a youth court or a justice, the judge shall

(a) cause the information to be read to him; and

(b) where the young person is not represented by counsel, inform him of his right to be so represented.

(2) A young person may waive the requirement under paragraph (1)(a) where the young person is represented by counsel.

(3) Where a young person is not represented in youth court by counsel, the youth court shall, before accepting a plea,

(a) satisfy itself that the young person understands the charge against him; and

(b) explain to the young person that he may plead guilty or not guilty to the charge.

(4) Where the youth court is not satisfied that a young person understands the charge against him, as required under paragraph (3)(a), the court shall enter a plea of not guilty on behalf of the young person and shall proceed with the trial in accordance with subsection 19(2).

PRE-DISPOSITION REPORT

Pre-Disposition report—Contents of report—Oral report with leave—Report to form part of record—Copies of pre-disposition report—Cross-examination —Report may be withheld from young person or private prosecutor—Report disclosed to other persons—Disclosure by the provincial director— Inadmissibility of statements.

14. (1) Where a youth court deems it advisable before making a disposition under section 20 in respect of a young person who is found guilty of an offence it may, and where a youth court is required under this Act to consider a pre-disposition report before making an order or a disposition in

respect of a young person it shall, require the provincial director to cause to be prepared a pre-disposition report in respect of the young person and to submit the report to the court.

(2) A pre-disposition report made in respect of a young person shall, subject to subsection (3), be in writing and shall include

(a) the results of an interview with the young person and, where reasonably possible, the results of an interview with the parents of the young person;

(b) the results of an interview with the victim in the case, where applicable and where reasonably possible; and

(c) such information as is applicable to the case including, where applicable,

(i) the age, maturity, character, behaviour and attitude of the young person and his willingness to make amends,

(ii) any plans put forward by the young person to change his conduct or to participate in activities or undertake measures to improve himself,

(iii) the history of previous findings of delinquency under the *Juvenile Delinquents Act* or previous findings of guilt under this or any other Act of Parliament or any regulation made thereunder or under an Act or the legislature of a province or any regulation made thereunder or by-law or ordinance of a municipality, the history of community or other services rendered to the young person with respect to such findings and the response of the young person to previous sentences or dispositions and to services rendered to him,

(iv) the history of alternative measures used to deal with the young persons and the response of the young person thereto,

(v) the availability of community services and facilities for young persons and the willingness of the young person to avail himself of such services or facilities,

(vi) the relationship between the young person and his parents and the degree of control and influence of the parents over the young persons, and

(vii) the school attendance and performance record and the employment record of the young person.

ADJUDICATION

Where young person pleads guilty—Where young person pleads not guilty— Application for transfer to ordinary court.

19. (1) Where a young person pleads guilty to an offence charged against him

and the youth court is satisfied that the facts support the charge, the court shall find the young person guilty of the offence.

(2) Where a young person pleads not guilty to an offence charged against him, or where a young person pleads guilty but the youth court is not satisfied that the facts support the charge, the court shall proceed with the trial and shall, after considering the matter, find the young person guilty or not guilty or make an order dismissing the charge, as the case may be.

(3) The court shall not make a finding under this section in respect of a young person in respect of whom an application may be made under section 16 for an order that the young person be proceeded against in ordinary court unless it has inquired as to whether any of the parties to the proceedings wishes to make such an application, and, if any party so wishes, has given that party an opportunity to do so. 1986, c. 32, s. 13.

DISPOSITIONS

Dispositions that may be made—Coming into force of disposition—Duration of disposition—Combined duration of dispositions—Duration of dispositions made at different times—Disposition continues when adult—Reasons for the disposition—Limitation on punishment—Application of Part XX of *Criminal Code*—Section 722 of *Criminal Code* does not apply—Contents of probation order.

20. (1) Where a youth court finds a young person guilty of an offence, it shall consider any pre-disposition report required by the court, any representations made by the parties to the proceedings or their counsel or agents and by the parents of the young person and any other relevant information before the court, and the court shall then make any one of the following dispositions, or any number thereof that are not inconsistent with each other:

(a) by order direct that the young person be discharged absolutely, if the court considers it to be in the best interests of the young person and not contrary to the public interest;

(b) impose on the young person a fine not exceeding one thousand dollars to be paid at such time and on such terms as the court may fix;

(c) order the young person to pay to any other person at such time and on such terms as the court may fix an amount by way of compensation for loss of or damage to property, for loss of income or support or for special damages for personal injury arising from the commission of the offence where the value thereof is readily ascertainable, but no order shall be made for general damages;

(d) order the young person to make restitution to any other person of any property obtained by the young person as a result of the commission of the offence within such time as the court may fix, if the property is owned by that other person or was, at the time of the offence, in his lawful possession;

(e) if any property obtained as a result of the commission of the offence has been sold to an innocent purchaser, where restitution of the property to its owner or any other person has been made of ordered, order the young person to pay the purchaser, at such time and on such terms as the court may fix, an amount not exceeding the amount paid by the purchaser for the property;

(f) subject to section 21, order the young person to compensate any person in kind or by way of personal services at such time and on such terms as the court may fix for any loss, damage or injury suffered by that person in respect of which an order may be made under paragraph (c) or (e);

(g) subject to section 21, order the young person to perform a community service at such time and on such terms as the court may fix;

(h) make any order of prohibition, seizure or forfeiture that may be imposed under any Act of Parliament or any regulation made thereunder where an accused is found guilty or convicted of that offence;

(i) subject to section 22, by order direct that the young person be detained for treatment, subject to such conditions as the court considers appropriate, in a hospital or other place where treatment is available, where a report has been made in respect of the young person pursuant to subsection 13(1) that recommends that the young person undergo treatment for a condition referred in paragraph 13(1)(e).

(j) place the young person on probation in accordance with section 23 for a specified period not exceeding two years;

(k) subject to section 24, commit the young person to custody, to be served continuously or intermittently, for a specified period not exceeding

(i) two years from the date of committal, or
(ii) where the young person is found guilty of an offence for which the punishment provided by the *Criminal Code* or any other Act of Parliament is imprisonment for life, three years from the date of committal; and

(l) impose on the young person such other reasonable and ancillary conditions as it deems advisable and in the best interest of the young person and the public.

EVIDENCE

General law on admissibility of statements to apply—When statements are admissible—Exception in certain cases for oral statements—Waiver of right to consult—Statements given under duress are inadmissible—Parent, etc., not a person in authority.

56. (1) Subject to this section, the law relating to the admissibility of statements made by persons accused of committing offences applies in respect of young persons.

(2) No oral or written statement given by a young person to a peace officer or other person who is, in law, a person in authority is admissible against the young person unless

(a) the statement was voluntary;

(b) the person to whom the statement was given has, before the statement was made, clearly explained to the young person, in language appropriate to his age and understanding, that

(i) the young person is under no obligation to give a statement,
(ii) any statement given by him may be used as evidence in proceedings against him,
(iii) the young person has the right to consult another person in accordance with paragraph (c), and
(iv) any statement made by the young person is required to be made in the presence of the person consulted, unless the young person desires otherwise;

(c) the young person has, before the statement was made, been given a reasonable opportunity to consult with counsel of a parent, or in the absence of a parent, an adult relative, or in the absence of a parent and an adult relative, any other appropriate adult chosen by the young person; and

(d) where the young person consults any person pursuant to paragraph (c), the young person has been given a reasonable opportunity to make the statement in the presence of that person.

PROTECTION OF PRIVACY OF YOUNG PERSONS

Identity Not to be Published—Limitation—Ex parte application for leave to publish—Order ceases to have effect—application for leave to publish —Contravention—Provincial court judge has absolute jurisdiction on indictment.

38. (1) Subject to this section, no person shall publish by any means any report

(a) of an offence committed or alleged to have been committed by a young person, unless an order has been made under section 16 with respect thereto, or

(b) of any hearing, adjudication, disposition or appeal concerning a young person who committed or is alleged to have committed an offence

in which the name of the young person, a child or a young person who is a victim of the offence or a child or a young person who appeared as a witness in connection with the offence, or in which any information serving to identify such young person or child, is disclosed.

(1.1) Subsection (1) does not apply in respect of the disclosure of information in the course of the administration of justice where it is not the purpose of the disclosure to make the information known in the community.

(1.2) A youth court judge shall, on the *ex parte* application of a peace officer, make an order permitting any person to publish a report described in subsection (1) that contains the name of a young person, or information serving to identify a young person, who has committed or is alleged to have committed an indictable offence, if the judge is satisfied that

(a) there is reason to believe that the young person is dangerous to others; and

(b) publication of the report is necessary to assist in apprehending the young person.

(1.3) An order made under subsection (1.2) shall cease to have effect two days after it is made.

(1.4) The youth court may, on the application of any person referred to in subsection (1), make an order permitting any person to publish a report in which the name of that person or information serving to identify that person, would be disclosed, if the court is satisfied that the publication of the report would not be contrary to the best interests of that person.

(2) Everyone who contravenes section (1)

(a) is guilty of an indictable offence and liable to imprisonment for a term not exceeding two years; or

(b) is guilty of an offence punishable on summary conviction.

(3) Where an accused is charged with an offence under paragraph (2)(a), a provincial court judge has absolute jurisdiction to try the case and his jurisdiction does not depend on the consent of the accused.

Appendix II

Table 1 Frequencies of Legal and Extra-Legal Variables

	CATEGORIES	N	PERCENTAGE
Dependent Variables			
Pre-appearance status	detained	476	30.8
	released	1,069	69.2
	TOTAL	1,545	
Plea	guilty	586	71.6
	not-guilty	233	28.4
	TOTAL	819	
Adjudication	conviction	528	86.6
	charge withdrawn	81	13.4
	TOTAL	609	
Disposition	unconditional release	206	32.4
	conditional release/incarceration	429	67.6
	TOTAL	635	
Independent Variables			
Race	White	949	72.8
	Native	233	17.9
	Other	121	9.3
Age	12–15	652	42.2
	16–18	893	57.8
Sex	male	1,310	83.5
	female	258	16.5
Family Presence	parent/guardian	736	57.9
	none	536	42.1
Counsel Status	private counsel	850	55.2
	duty counsel	691	44.8
Record	previous conviction	489	65.4
	no record	259	34.6
Seriousness of Offence	serious	602	74.0
	non-serious	212	26.0

References

Aday, David P., Jr
1986 'Court Structure, Defense Attorney Use and Juvenile Court Decisions', *Sociological Quarterly* 27(1): 107-9.

Ariès, Philippe
1962 *Centuries of Childhood*. New York: Random House.

Arnold, William
1971 'Race and Ethnicity Relative to Other Factors in Juvenile Court Dispositions', *American Journal of Sociology* 77: 211-27.

Baker, R.J. and J.A. Nelder
1978 *General Linear Interactive Modeline*. Release 3. Oxford: Numerical Alforithms Group.

Bala, N. and R. Corrado
1985 *Juvenile Justice in Canada: A Comparative Study*. Ottawa: Programs Branch, Solicitor General of Canada.

Barnhorst, S.
1980 'Female Delinquency and Sex-Role Stereotype', Doctoral diss., Queen's University, Kingston.

Barrett, M. and M. McIntosh
1982 *The Anti-Social Family*. London: Verso/New Left.

Bishop, Donna M., and Charles E. Frazier
1988 'The Influence of Race in Juvenile Justice Processing', *Journal of Research in Crime and Delinquency* 25: 242-63.

Black, Donald J. and Albert Reiss
1970 'Police Control of Juveniles', *American Sociological Review* 35: 63-77.

Blumberg, S.
1979 *Criminal Justice*. New York: New Viewpoints.

Boldt, E., L. Hursh, S. Johnson, and M. Taylor
1983 'Presentence Reports and the Incarceration of Natives', *Canadian Journal of Criminology* 25: 269-75.

Bradford, J.M.W.
1988 'Organic Treatment for the Male Sexual Offender' in R.A. Prentky and V.L. Quinsey (eds), *Human Sexual Aggression: Current Perspectives*. Annals of the New York Academy of Sciences, 528: 193-202.

Brannigan, Augustine
1984 *Crime, Courts, and Corrections*. Toronto: Holt, Rinehart and Winston.

Brantingham, Patricia L.
1985 'Sentencing Disparity: An Analysis of Judicial Consistency', *Journal of Quantitative Criminology* 1(3): 281-305.

Campbell, A.
1981 *Girl Delinquents*. Oxford: Basil Blackwell.

Caputo, Tullio
1991 'Pleasing Everybody Please Nobody: Changing the Juvenile Justice System in Canada' in Les Samuelson and Bernard Schissel (eds), *Criminal Justice: Sentencing Issues and Reforms*. Toronto: Garamond Press.

Caputo, Tullio and Denis C. Bracken
1988 'Custodial Dispositions and the Young Offenders Act' in Joe Hudson, Joseph P. Hornick, and Barbara Burrows (eds), *Justice and the Young Offender in Canada*. Toronto: Wall and Thompson.

Carrigan, D. Owen
1991 *Crime and Punishment in Canada: A History*. Toronto: McClelland and Stewart.

Carrington, Peter and Sharon Moyer
1990 'The Effect of Defence Counsel on Plea and Outcome in Juvenile Court', *Canadian Journal of Criminology* 32: 621-37.

Casey, M. *et al.*
1966 'Sex Chromosome Abnormalities in Two State Hospitals for Patients Requiring Special Security'. *Nature* 5: 641-3

Chambliss, William
1969 *Crime and the Legal Process*. New York: McGraw-Hill.
——— and Robert B. Seidman
1971 *Law, Order and Power*. Reading, Mass.: Addison-Wesley.

Chunn, D.E.
1990 'Boys Will be Men, Girls Will be Mothers: The Legal Regulation of Childhood in Toronto and Vancouver', *Sociological Studies of Childhood* 3: 87-110.

Cicourel, Aaron
1968 *The Social Organization of Juvenile Justice*. New York: John Wiley and Sons.

Cohen, Lawrence E., and James R. Kluegel
1979 'Selecting Delinquents for Adjudication: An Analysis of Intake Screening Decision in Two Metropolitan Juvenile Courts', *Journal of Research in Crime and Delinquency* 16: 143-63.

Comack, Elizabeth
1991 'We Will Get Some Good Out of this Riot Yet: The Canadian State, Drug Legislation and Class Conflict' in E. Comack and S. Brickey (eds), *The Social Basis of Law: Critical Readings in the Sociology of Law*. Toronto: Garamond Press.

Conrad, Klaus
1963 *Der Konstitutionstypus*. Berlin: Springer Verlag.

Corrado, Raymond, Marc LeBlanc, and Jean Trepanier
1983 *Current Issues in Juvenile Justice*. Toronto: Butterworths

Cruikshank, Julie
1981 'Matrifocal Families in the Canadian North' in K. Ishwaran (ed.), *The Canadian Family*. Toronto: Holt, Rinehart and Winston.
Cusson, Maurice
1983 *Why Delinquency?* Toronto: University of Toronto Press.
Dahrendorf, Ralph
1959 *Class and Class Conflict in Industrial Society*. Stanford: Stanford University Press.
Dannefer, D., and R. Shutt
1982 'Race and Juvenile Justice Processing in Court and Police Agencies', *American Journal of Sociology* 87: 1113-32.
Denno, Deborah and Ruth Schwartz
1985 *Biological, Psychological, and Environmental Factors in Delinquency and Mental Illness*. Westport, Conn.: Greenwood Press.
Department of Justice
1965 *Juvenile Delinquency in Canada, The Report of the Department of Justice Committee on Juvenile Delinquency*. Ottawa: Queen's Printer.
Donzelot, J.
1979 *The Policing of Families*. New York: Random House.
Doob, Anthony
1993 'Trends in the Use of Custodial Dispositions for Young Offenders' in Thomas O'Reilly-Fleming and Barry Clark (eds), *Youth Injustice: Canadian Perspectives*. Toronto: Canadian Scholars' Press.
——— and Lucien A. Beaulieu
1993 'Variation in the Exercise of Judicial Discretion with Young Offenders' in Thomas O'Reilly-Fleming and Barry Clark (eds), *Youth Injustice: Canadian Perspectives*. Toronto: Canadian Scholars' Press.
——— and Janet B.L. Chan
1983 'Factors Affecting Police Decisions to Take Juveniles to Court', *Canadian Journal of Criminology* 24: 447-62.
Dootjes, Inez, Patricia Erickson, and Richard Fox
1972 'Defence Counsel in Juvenile Court: A Variety of Roles', *Canadian Journal of Criminology and Corrections* 14(2): 132-49.
Elliot, D.S. and S. Ageton
1980 'Reconciling Race and Class Differences in Self-reported and Official Estimates of Delinquency', *American Sociological Review* 45: 95-110.
Ericson, Richard V.
1982 *Reproducing Order: A Study of Police Patrol Work*. Toronto: University of Toronto Press.
——— and Patricia Baranek
1986 'The Reordering of Justice' in Neil Boyd (ed.), *The Social Dimensions of Law*. Scarborough, Ont.: Prentice-Hall.
Erickson, P.
1975 'Legalistic and Traditional Role Expectations for Defence Counsel in Juvenile Court'. *Canadian Journal of Criminology and Corrections* 17: 79-93.
Eysenck, H.J.
1977 *Crime and Personality*. London: Routledge and Kegan Paul.
Farrington, D.P.
1979 *Juvenile Justice in England and Canada*. Ottawa: Solicitor General.

Feld, Barry C.
1989 'The Right to Counsel in Juvenile Court: An Empirical Study of When Lawyers Appear and the Difference They Make', *Journal of Criminal Law and Criminology* 79(4): 1185-1346.

Ferdinand, T.N. and L.G. Lechterhand
1970 'Inner-city Youth, the Police, the Juvenile Court and Justice', *Social Problems* 17: 510-26.

Fitz, J.
1979 'The Child as a Legal Subject' in R. Dale, G. Esland, R. Fergusson, and M. McDonald (eds), *Education and the State*, vol. II, *Politics, Patriarchy and Practice*. Milton Keynes, England: Open University Press.

Foucault, Michel
1979 *Discipline and Punishment: The Birth of the Prison*. New York: Vintage Books.

Fowler, Kevin
1993 'Youth Gangs: Criminals, Thrillseekers or the New Voice of Anarchy?' in Thomas O'Reilly Fleming and Barry Clark (eds), *Youth Injustice: Canadian Perspectives*. Toronto: Canadian Scholars' Press.

Fox, Richard G.
1987 'Controlling Sentencers', *Australian and New Zealand Journal of Criminology* 20: 218-46.

Frechette, M., and M. Leblanc
1978 *La Delinquance Cachée des Adolescents Montréalais* Rapport final, vol. 1. Université de Montréal: Groupe de Recherche sur l'Inadaptation Juvenile.

Gagnon, R. and L. Biron
1979 *Les Filles Marginalisées: Perspective Statistique*. Rapport no. 1. Université de Montréal: Groupe de Recherche sur l'Inadaptation Juvenile.

Geller, G.
1987 'Young Women in Conflict with the Law' in E. Adelberg and C. Currie (eds), *Too Few to Count: Canadian Women in Conflict with the Law*. Vancouver: Press Gang.

———
1980 'The Streaming of Males and Females in the Juvenile Court Clinic.' Doctoral diss., Ontario Institute for Studies in Education, University of Toronto.

Gibbons, Don C.
1987 *Society, Crime, and Criminal Behavior*. Englewood Cliffs: Prentice-Hall.

Gilbert, Nigel
1981 *Modelling Society: An Introduction to Loglinear Analysis for Social Researchers*. London: George Allen and Unwin.

Glueck, S. and E. Glueck
1950 *Unraveling Juvenile Delinquency*. Cambridge: Harvard University Press.

Goldman, Nathan
1963 'The Differential Selection of Juvenile Offenders for Court Appearance', *National Council on Crime and Delinquency*.

Goodwin, Donald W.
1986 'Studies of Familial Alcoholism: A Growth Industry.' In Donald W. Goodwin, Katherine Teilman Van Dusen, and Sarnoff A. Mednick (eds), *Longitudinal Research in Alcoholism*. Boston: Kluwer Academic Publishers Group.

Green, Melvyn
1986 'The History of Canadian Narcotics Legislation: The Formative Years' in Neil Boyd (ed.), *The Social Dimensions of Law*. Scarborough, Ont.: Prentice-Hall.

Griffiths, Curt T. and Simon Verdun-Jones
1989 *Canadian Criminal Justice*. Toronto: Butterworths.

Hackler, Jim and W. Paranjape
1984 'Official Reactions to Juvenile Theft: Comparisons Across Provinces', *Canadian Journal of Criminology* 26: 179-99.

Hagan, John
1974 'Extra-Legal Attributes and Criminal Sentencing: An Assessment of a Sociological Viewpoint', *Law and Society Review* 8: 357-83.

———, A. Roald Gillis, and Janet Chan
1980 'Explaining Official Delinquency: A Spatial Study of Class, Conflict and Control' in Robert Silverman and James J. Teevan, Jr (eds), *Crime in Canadian Society*. Toronto: Butterworths.

——— and Jeffrey Leon
1977 'Rediscovering Delinquency: Social History, Political Ideology, and the Sociology of Law', *American Sociological Review* 42: 587-98.

Hamilton, A.C. and Murray Sinclair
1991 *Manitoba Aboriginal Justice Inquiry*. Winnipeg: Government of Manitoba.

Havemann, Paul
1992 'Crisis Justice for Youth: Making the Young Offenders Act and the Discourse of Penalty' in Dawn Currie and Brian MacLean (eds), *Rethinking the Administration of Justice*. Halifax: Fernwood.

Hepburn, John R.
1978 'Race and the Decision to Arrest: An Analysis of Warrants Issued', *Journal of Research in Crime and Delinquency* 15: 54-73

Heumann, Milton
1978 *Plea Bargaining: The Experiences of Prosecutors, Judges, and Defense Attorneys*. Chicago: University of Chicago Press.

Hindelang, M.J.
1973 'Causes of Delinquency: A Partial Replication and Extension', *Social Problems* 20(4): 471-87.

——— and Travis Hirschi
1979 'Correlates of Delinquency: The Illusion of Discrepancy Between Self-report and Official Measures', *American Sociological Review* 44: 995-1014.

———, Travis Hirschi, and J.G. Weis
1982 *Measuring Delinquency*. Beverly Hills: Sage.

Hirschi, Travis
1969 *Causes of Delinquency*. Los Angeles: University of California Press.

———
1975 'Labelling Theory and Juvenile Delinquency: An Assessment of the Evidence' in W. Gove (ed.), *The Labelling of Deviance*. New York: Halsted Press.

Hogarth, John
1971 *Sentencing as a Human Process*. Toronto: University of Toronto Press.

Huizinga, David and Delbert S. Elliot
1987 'Juvenile Offenders: Prevalence, Offender Incidence, and Arrest Rates by Race', *Crime and Delinquency* 33(2): 206-23.

Hylton, John
1981 'Some Attitudes Towards Natives in a Prairie City', *Canadian Journal of Criminology* 23: 357-63.

Jackson, Margaret A. and Curt T. Griffiths
1991 *Canadian Criminology: Perspectives on Crime and Criminality*. Toronto: Harcourt Brace Jovanovich.

Jackson, Michael
1989 'Locking Up Natives in Canada', *University of British Columbia Law Review* 23(2): 215-300.

Klein, Malcolm
1976 'Issues and Realities in Police Diversion Programs', *Crime and Delinquency* 22: 421-7.

Knight, R.A.
1988 'A Taxonomic Analysis of Child Molesters' in R.A. Prentky and V.L. Quinsey (eds), *Human Sexual Aggression: Current Perspectives*. Annals of the New York Academy of Sciences, 528: 2-20.

——— and R.A. Prentky
1987 'Motivational Components in a Taxonomy for Rapists: A Validational Analysis', *Criminal Justice and Behaviour* 13: 141-64.

Knoke, David and Peter J. Burke
1986 *Log-linear Models*. London: Sage Publications.

Kueneman, Rod and Rick Linden
1983 'Factors Affecting Dispositions in the Winnipeg Juvenile Court' in Raymond Corrado, Marc LeBlanc, and Jean Trepanier (eds), *Current Issues in Juvenile Justice*. Toronto: Butterworths.

Laing, R.D.
1983 *The Politics of the Family*. Toronto: CBC Enterprises.

Landau, S.F.
1981 'Juveniles and the Police: Who Is Charged Immediately and Who Is Referred to the Juvenile Bureau', *British Journal of Criminology* 21: 27-46.

Langley, M., B. Thomas, and R. Parkinson
1978 'Youths' Expectations and Perceptions of Their Initial Juvenile Court Experience', *Canadian Journal of Criminology* 20(1): 43-53.

LaPrairie, Carol Pitcher
1988 'The Young Offenders Act and Aboriginal Youth' in Joe Hudson, Joseph Hornick, and Barbara Burrows (eds), *Justice and the Young Offender in Canada*. Toronto: Wall and Thompson.

———
1983 'Native Juveniles in Court: Some Preliminary Observations' in Thomas Fleming and L.A. Visano (eds)., *Deviant Designations: Crime, Law, and Deviance*. Toronto: Butterworths.

——— and C.T. Griffiths
1982 'Native Indian Delinquency: A Review of Recent Findings', *Native People and Justice in Canada*, Special Issue, Part 1. *Canadian Legal Aid Bulletin* 5(01): 39-46.

Law Reform Commission of Canada
1991 *Report on Aboriginal Peoples and Criminal Justice*. Ottawa: Minister of Justice, Canada.

LeBlanc, Marc
1983 'Delinquency as an Epiphenomenon of Adolescence' in R. Corrado, M. LeBlanc, and J. Trepanier (eds), *Current Issues in Juvenile Justice*. Toronto: Butterworths.

Lemert, Edwin
1967 *Human Deviance, Social Problems, and Social Control*. Englewood Cliffs, N.J.: Prentice-Hall.

Leschied, A. and P. Jaffe
1987 'Impact of the Young Offenders Act on Court Dispositions: A Comparative Analysis', *Canadian Journal of Criminology* 30: 421-30.

Lundman, Richard L., R.E. Sykes, and John P. Clark
1978 'Police Control of Juveniles-Replication', *Journal of Research in Crime and Delinquency* 15(1): 74-91.

Magnussen, D., H. Stattin, and A. Duner
1983 'Aggression and Criminality in a Longitudinal Perspective' in K.T. Van Dusen and S.A. Mednick (eds), *Prospective Studies of Crime and Delinquency*. Boston: Kluwer-Nijhoff.

Mandel, Michael
1986 'Democracy, Class and Canadian Sentencing Law' in Stephen Brickey and Elizabeth Comack (eds), *The Social Basis of Law: Critical Readings in the Sociology of Law*. Toronto: Garamond Press.

Markwart, A.E. and R.R. Corrado
1989 'Is the Young Offenders Act More Punitive?' in L.A. Beaulieu (ed.), *Young Offender Dispositions: Perspectives on Principles and Practices*. Toronto: Wall and Thompson.

Marshal, Ineke Haen and Charles W. Thomas
1983 'Discretionary Decision-Making and the Juvenile Court', *Juvenile and Family Court Journal* 34(3): 47-59.

Matza, Graham
1964 *Delinquency and Drift*. New York: Wiley.

McCarthy, Belinda R. and Brent L. Smith
1986 'The Conceptualization of Discrimination in the Juvenile Justice Process: The Impact of Administrative Factors and Screening Decisions On Juvenile Court Dispositions', *Criminology* 24(1): 41-64.

Meyer, Philippe
1977 *The Child and the State: the Intervention of the State in Family Life*. Cambridge: Cambridge University Press.

Murphy, Emily
1922 *The Black Candle*. Toronto: Thomas Allen.

Myers, Martha A.
1987 'Economic Inequality and Discrimination in Sentencing', *Social Forces* 65(3): 746-66.

Olweus, D.
1983 'Testosterone in the Development of Aggressive Antisocial Behaviour in Adolescents' in K.T. Van Dusen and S.A. Mednick (eds), *Prospective Studies of Crime and Delinquency*. Boston: Kluwer-Nijhoff.

Piliavin, Irving and Scott Briar
1964 'Police Encounters With Juveniles', *American Journal of Sociology* 70: 206-14.

Platt, Anthony
1969   *The Child Savers: The Invention of Delinquency*. Chicago: University of Chicago Press.
Pollock, V.E. and J. Volavka, D.W. Goodwin, S.A. Mednick, W.F. Gabrielli, J. Knop, and F. Schulsinger
1983   'The EEG After Alcoholism Administration in Men at Risk for Alcoholism'. *Archives of General Psychiatry* 40: 857-61.
Pollock, V.E., T.W. Teasdale, W.F. Gabrielli, and J.Knop
1986   'Subjective and Objective Measures of Response to Alcohol among Young Men at Risk for Alcoholism', *Journal of Studies on Alcohol* 47: 297-304.
Price, W. *et al.*
1967   'Behavioural Disorders and Patterns among XXY Males Identified at a Maximum Security Hospital'.
Quinney, Richard
1977   *Class, State and Crime*. New York: David McKay.
Reid-MacNevin, Susan
1991   'A Theoretical Understanding of Current Canadian Juvenile-justice Policy' in Alan Leschied, Peter Jaffe, and Wayne Willis (eds), *The Young Offenders Act: A Revolution in Canadian Juvenile Justice*. Toronto: University of Toronto Press.
Ross, Rupert
1992   *Dancing With the Ghost: Exploring Indian Reality*. Markham, Ontario: Octopus Publishing Group.
Samuelson, Les and Bernard Schissel
1991   *Criminal Justice: Sentencing Issues and Reform*. Toronto: Garamond Press.
Sarbin, Theodore and Jeffrey E. Miller
1970   'Demonism Revisited: The Chromosomal Anomaly', *Issues in Criminology* 5: 195-207.
Sebald, Robert
1968   *Adolescence: a Sociological Analysis*. Englewood Cliffs: Prentice-Hall.
Sellin, Thorsten and Marvin Wolfgang
1964   *The Measurement of Delinquency*. New York: John Wiley and Sons.
Shah, Saleem A. and Loren H. Roth
1974   'Biological and Psychophysiological Factors in Criminology' in Daniel Glaser (ed.), *Handbook of Criminology*. Chicago: Rand McNally.
Shearing, Clifford D.
1981   *Organizational Police Deviance*. Toronto: Butterworths.
Sheldon, William
1949   *Varieties of Delinquent Youth: An Introduction to Constitutional Psychiatry*. New York: Harper and Row.
Sutherland, N.
1976   *Children in English-Canadian Society: Framing the Twentieth-Century Consensus*. Toronto: University of Toronto Press.
Taylor, Ian, Paul Walton, and Jock Young
1973   *The New Criminology*. New York: Basic Books.
Thomas, C. and C. Seiverdes
1975   'Juvenile Court Intake: An Analysis of Discretionary Decision-Making', *Criminology* 12: 413-32.

Thomas, C.W. and S.M. Fitch
1981   'The Exercise of Discretion in the Juvenile Justice System', *Juvenile and Family Court Journal* 32(1): 31-50.
Thornberry, Terence
1973   'Race, Socio-Economic Status and Sentencing in the Juvenile Justice System', *Journal of Criminal Law and Criminology* 64: 90-8.

——
1979   'Sentencing Disparities in the Juvenile Justice System', *Journal of Criminal Law and Criminology* 70: 164-71.
Turk, Austin T.
1969   *Criminality and the Legal Order*. Chicago: Rand McNally.
Webber, Marlene
1991   *Street Kids: The Tragedy of Canada's Runaways*. Toronto: University of Toronto Press.
West, Gordon
1991   'Towards a More Socially Informed Understanding of Canadian Delinquency Legislation' in Alan Leschied, Peter Jaffe, and Wayne Willis (eds), *The Young Offenders Act: A Revolution in Canadian Juvenile Justice*. Toronto: University of Toronto Press.

——
1984   *Young Offenders and the State: A Canadian Perspective on Delinquency*. Toronto: Butterworths.
Wilkins, James L.
1976   *Legal Aid in the Criminal Courts*. Toronto: University of Toronto Press.
Williams, J.R. and M. Gold
1972   'From Delinquent Behaviour to Official Delinquency', *Social Problems* 20: 209-28.
Wilson, Margo and Martin Daly
1985   'Competitiveness, Risk Taking, and Violence: The Young Male Syndrome', *Ethology and Sociobiology* 6: 59-73.
Wynne, D. and T. Hartnagel
1975   'Plea Negotiation in Canada', *Canadian Journal of Criminology and Corrections* 17: 45-56.
Yerbury, J. Colin and Curt T. Griffiths
1991   'Minorities, Crime, and the Law' in Margaret A. Jackson and Curt T. Griffiths (eds), *Canadian Criminology: Perspectives on Crime and Delinquency*. Toronto: Harcourt Brace Jovanovich.
York, Geoffrey
1991   'Defence of the North: The Native Economy and Land Claims' in E. Comack and S. Brickey (eds), *The Social Basis of Law: Critical Readings in the Sociology of Law*. Toronto: Garamond Press.
Zatz, Marjorie S.
1987   'The Changing Forms of Racial/Ethnic Biases in Sentencing', *Journal of Research in Crime and Delinquency* 24(1): 69-92.

Index

8539